The Panera Bread Cookbook

The Panera Bread Cookbook

Breadmaking Essentials and Recipes from America's Favorite Bakery-Cafe

By the Panera Bread Team   Foreword by Peter Reinhart   Recipes by Ward Bradshaw and Joel Cammett

Clarkson Potter/Publishers
New York

Copyright © 2004 by Panera Bread.
Photographs by Jay Baker, Bill Bettencourt, and
Steve Pelosi.
Illustrations by Arlene Ligori

Published by Clarkson Potter/Publishers, New York,
New York.
Member of the Crown Publishing Group,
a division of Random House, Inc.
www.crownpublishing.com

CLARKSON N. POTTER is a trademark and POTTER and
colophon are registered trademarks of Random House, Inc.

Printed in the United States of America

Design by Jennifer K. Beal

Library of Congress Cataloging-in-Publication Data
Bradshaw, Ward.
    The Panera Bread cookbook : breadmaking essentials
and recipes from America's favorite bakery-cafe / the
Panera Bread team ; foreword by Peter Reinhart ; recipes
by Ward Bradshaw and Joel Cammett.
        Includes index.
    1. Bread.   I. Cammett, Joel.   II. Panera Bread (Cafe).
III. Title.
TX769.B768   2004
641.8'15—dc22   2004011612

ISBN 1-4000-8041-X

10   9   8   7   6   5

First Edition

Panera Bread dedicates this cookbook to our customers. Thank you for welcoming us into your neighborhoods, sharing your stories, and helping us celebrate fresh and authentic foods. We cherish our role as your community gathering place, and will continue to strive to make our bakery-cafes the perfect environment for breaking bread with friends and family.

Contents

Building a Bread Culture in America

Peter Reinhart

On the first day of my five-week bread class at the International Baking and Pastry Institute of Johnson and Wales University, I tell my students that their mission as bakers will be to evoke the full potential of flavor trapped in the grain. They will do this by learning and mastering the twelve stages of breadmaking and then over the next few days, in addition to making bread with them, I tell them stories about bread. By the end of the five weeks, their relationship with bread—their connection to it—is changed forever.

Bread has a story to tell.

For instance, when the youngest child at the Passover seder asks, "Why is this night different from all other nights?" it begins a process of transmission that runs right through bread, as one of the follow-up questions is, "On all other nights we eat leavened bread, why on this night do we eat only unleavened bread?" An elder then tells the story of the Hebrews' escape from bondage in Egypt. As they fled, they spared just enough time to make bread but could not afford time for bread to rise. What the elder does not say, because it is just a very subtle underlayer of the story, is that Egypt was the proud creator of leavened bread. Their civilization gets the credit for figuring out how to ferment grain, apply heat, and transform a beerlike substance into something that we now call bread. Unleavened bread, matzo as we call it, was considered an inferior product, a humble antecedent to its more exalted leavened counterpart. Yet in this story, the exalted masters were brought down by their enslaved, humble, matzo-eating servants. The great, leavened culture of Egypt was, at least for a short time, trumped by the unleavened renegades. Bread has many such stories to tell.

When Marie Antoinette offered her famous apocryphal last words, *not* "Let them eat cake," but more properly translated, "Let them eat brioche," she illustrated, yet again, the special connection that people have to their bread. In France, by 1790, brioche had become a symbol of the aristocracy since it was made with expensive butter and eggs that made it too costly for the masses. Bakers tried to appease their poorer customers by offering a less buttery, less expensive version, nicknamed poor man's brioche, but it was too late to save poor Queen Marie. Perhaps if she had found a way to distribute the full-fat version a little earlier in her reign . . . well, who knows?

When I visited the city of Bologna a few years ago, the local people told me, "You are the bread man, so you must try our special bread, the *manino,* our hand-bread." I thought they meant bread shaped by hand but what they actually meant was bread in the shape of a hand, complete with five fingers. When I tasted it I had to hide my disappointment because it did not taste particularly good. I thought maybe I had been given a stale piece, so I asked a friend, a writer of books on Italian breads, if this was typical or just a bad example. She assured me it was typical and that it was not, by our current standards, the best-tasting bread. "But," she warned, "don't try to tell that to the locals. They are quite proud of it."

Indeed, the Bolognese have a special connection with their bread that supercedes its taste. It is a local tradition, unique to the immediate countryside—bread with its own legendary status. You don't dishonor such traditions by pointing out that the bread could be improved by fermenting it longer or by tweaking the formula. Traditions and stories such as these play a pivotal role in every bread culture.

What exactly is a bread culture? If we were to look at culture from a culinary perspective we could argue that Americans live in a burger culture. Where I'm from in Philadelphia I know there is a cheesesteak subculture. In some regions, like in the San Francisco Bay Area, we clearly have an established sourdough subculture that has served as a catalyst of sorts toward what has been slowly growing into a broader national bread culture. Just ten years ago, who could have known that small bakery-cafes baking artisan breads were the beginning of a major trend? What began in small neighborhoods inspired the growth of places like Panera Bread, bringing the artisan traditions to the rest of America.

One thing we can assert is that in today's America we have a well-developed pizza culture, as I discovered in my travels while researching a book on the subject. During my adventures in pursuit of pizza that exemplified the highest standards of excellence, I met one pizza maker, a *pizzaiolo* as he would be called in Italy, who gave me an insight into how people can connect with a culture through food.

Chris Bianco has a restaurant in Phoenix, Arizona, called Pizzeria Bianco. He has become known among many serious pizza hunters, like me, as possibly the finest *pizzaiolo* in America. In one of our conversations there was a moment of enlightenment when I asked him what made his pizzas better than everyone else's.

"Many people have asked me that," Chris replied, "and have even wanted to give me money to open branches of Pizzeria Bianco in Las Vegas and other cities. They want to take it national. They want me to teach other *pizzaioli* all my secrets. But they don't understand. They think I have all these secret tricks, and I do have some pretty good tricks, but that's not the point. That's not the secret to my pizza. The secret to my pizza is not the tomatoes, though I am picky about those and am extremely proud of the growers I purchase all my produce from. It's not the cheese, even though I do make it myself every day. It's not the wood-fired oven, though the pizza wouldn't be as good without it. People ask for my secrets, but I think it might be a disservice to give out so-called cooking secrets. They might think these tricks are the key to my pizza, but they're not. Here's the secret, and I hope this doesn't sound vain or conceited. The secret is . . ."

He was having trouble finishing his sentence, although I knew what he was going to say.

"The secret is, well, it's *me*. I'm the secret. It's my passion, my energy, my commitment. I can't bottle that and give it to someone else. Maybe someone else has the talent and the passion and I could teach them the formulas, but, really, there aren't too many people who feel the way I do, who care as much as I care. I can remember nearly every pizza I ever made, and what many of my customers had the last time they were here, and I try to make decisions to make it right for each of them. Has every pizza been perfect? No. I'm still working on getting it perfect. I don't know if I ever will, but sometimes I really nail one. When people come into my restaurant, what I really want is for them to say, 'Why don't you pick out the pizza you think I should have?' I want them to trust me to choose the exact right one for them. I like it when people trust me to read them and match them up with the perfect choice. That makes me feel like I'm connecting with them."

What I realized more deeply than ever after talking with Chris is that *connectedness* is a powerful and essential part of culture. In a culture we always find people who have achieved a form of connectedness, and they transmit this connectedness through their artisanship. Sometimes this transmission is done through formal education, but often it is done through celebration, through festivals, music, dance, stories, and always, always through food. And where there is food, we also find some kind of bread at the very heart of a celebration or festival. Why? Because it works on so many levels; bread tells a story.

When I teach my students how to evoke the full potential of flavor trapped in grain, I explain to them that what separates bread from all other foods is that it is a transformational food. Unlike in regular cooking, where the ingredients were once alive and then harvested and recombined with other ingredients to make something new, bread baking is different. With bread, we take ingredients that were once alive and then harvested, such as wheat, and we bring them back to life. The bread is transformed through the process we call leavening, a word whose very root means to enliven. The changing of clay made from flour, salt, and water into dough, through the infusion of leaven, represents a transformation from dead to alive; it does not get much more radical than that in the kitchen.

Not only is there a transformation from dead to alive, but later, this now living organism called dough is formed by the baker into individual loaves and there is a second transformation, as this living dough goes into the oven. The leaven, having accomplished its mission, gives up its life as the dough bakes. What emerges from the oven is radically different from what went in; living dough, as it dies, is transformed into something we now call bread. Dough, as alive as it may be, is not something we would eat, but when it is transformed into bread it is not only beautiful, but it nourishes us. Is it any wonder that bread has served in all cultures as a sacred symbol for life?

I call this transformational process the leaven factor, and have found it to be a powerful metaphor with many applications. This elaboration of bread into the metaphorical realm helps my students, I believe, to connect with bread in a deeper way, as they mature both as students of the culinary arts and also as human beings. They will become, in time, the next generation of storytellers, and they also will become the leaven factors for others.

When I was their age I lived in what we now call the turbulent counter-culture of the late 1960s. One of my first causes, and the beginning of my own spiritual and culinary awakening, revolved around the notion that white flour and white sugar were the enemy. Adele Davis was one of our iconic figures and she championed whole grains. What we called the back-to-the-earth movement was symbolized by whole-grain bread. Years later I identified this as the first wave of the bread revolution, a revolution that took three waves and nearly thirty years to unfold. The first phase, this whole-grain wave, reached a small but influential segment of society and planted scattered seeds of political and cultural influence.

The second phase occurred in the 1970s as Americans, on a larger scale, became more aware of European culinary influences, including traditional bread methodology. American bakers and chefs were going to Europe, and European chefs and bakers were coming to America, sharing knowledge and raising the culinary bar. Instead of finding a basket of mass-produced soft rolls or stale French bread on the table, patrons at the finer dining establishments expected to find fresh, crusty bread of world-class quality, sometimes made by a local artisan baker and sometimes made right in the restaurant. This phase, the traditional wave, is characterized by the recognition of artisanship and time honored advanced fermentation techniques to produce bread of the highest quality.

By the mid-1980s the paradigm of excellent bread was beginning to take hold, which led to a third phase, the neo-traditional wave. In this wave the combination of European fermentation techniques, combined with unrestrained American creativity in distinctively regional applications, brought the bread revolution into mass markets. A major sign of this is the proliferation of bakery-cafes, like Panera Bread, making and serving fresh bread representative of a synthesis of all three waves. The reemergence of mass interest in whole-grain breads in response to the low-carbohydrate movement is yet another example of the visionary insight by the voices of the first wave, seeds planted forty years ago at last bearing fruit.

In the 1800s nearly 80 percent of bread in America was made in home ovens. When high-speed mechanized baking systems took over in the early to mid-1900s the balance shifted, and, until recently, very few Americans knew the pleasure of the aroma of fresh-baked bread in their own homes. At the end of the twentieth century, bread machines hit the scene at about the same time as the emergence of the artisan bakery movement, and neighborhood bakery-cafes like Panera Bread introduced European-quality bread to a growing number of people. It seemed as though we were on the cusp of a true bread renaissance.

Yet now we face what is perhaps the first real challenge to this bread renaissance as we enter an era of anticarbohydrate mania. There is suddenly fear and doubt in the air about the nutritional value of bread and we may need to ask, "Why is this night different from all other nights? On recent nights we ate bread with a free conscience as we discovered the joys of bread long heralded by our European culinary elders. Why now, on this night, do people want me to feel guilty in my complex-carbohydrate pleasure?"

Dietitians know that people in this country are not obese because they eat bread. The Europeans and Greeks have historically eaten two to three times the amount of bread we eat, per capita, and only recently have they begun to experience the obesity problems that we have in America, and their bread consumption has actually gone down. Americans aren't obese because they eat too many burger buns with their shakes and fries at fast-food restaurants, or too many bagels with their cream cheese schmears. We intuitively and scientifi-cally know that in the long run the only dietary plan that will emerge as sound and healthy is called balance, or moderation in all things.

Bread and carbohydrates are not the enemy. We all know, or ought to know, that excess is the true enemy of proper nutrition.

We can see that the recent round of low-carbohydrate diets represents an extreme corrective to an extreme disease, and we know from experience that, in time, the pendulum will swing the other way and eventually find a point of balance for each person. Those who are spinning the scary carbohydrate stories may not be friends of bread bakers, but they may be doing us a huge favor. They have created a buzz that has brought us to a point, long overdue, of valid and proper concern. We bread bakers may not necessarily come up with all the answers, but perhaps we can begin to identify the right questions. And as we do we will tell our story, our many stories, because when the youngest at the table asks us to explain whether bread is bad for us or good for us, or what is the rightful place of bread in our lives, we can frame our answers in many ways and on many levels. We have many bread stories to tell.

Regardless of the stories we choose to tell, I hope one thing we will convey to those whom we know and love is that bread has been here and has played a major role in humanity for six thousand years. It definitely is not going away. After six thousand years of bread as a universal metaphor for life and for transformation, we bread bakers don't react; we transmit. We even create an ever-growing number of new venues for transmission, the cafes where we can tell our stories in words and through the bread itself. We celebrate with and through bread; we evoke the full potential of flavor trapped in the grain. We transmit the story; we connect. In so doing, we continue to make our contributions, as we always have and always will, to the greater good.

Bringing the Artisan Tradition Home

Since opening our first bakery-cafe in 1987, Panera Bread has created something special in neighborhoods across America. At a time when few people outside of major metropolitan areas had access to bakery-fresh bread, Panera set out to make high-quality, handcrafted loaves available on a broad scale. Each day, in every location, Panera Bread bakers take natural ingredients and craft loaves for all to enjoy. From our signature Sourdough to our Three Seed, from our Cinnamon Raisin to our Stone-Milled Rye, Panera's skilled bakers take pride in each loaf of bread that leaves the oven. The incredible success of Panera proves that bread remains one of the most popular and culturally significant foods in the world. Diet and dining trends may come and go, but bread continues to be a prominent fixture on our dinner tables, and an important symbol of friendship and community. In fact, every time Panera opens a new bakery-cafe, we hold a special "bread breaking" ceremony to celebrate with our new neighbors.

Today American foods are changing to reflect the resurgence of artisan breads. Once relegated to the background of our favorite dishes, bread has moved to the forefront with its bold flavors and textures. Specialty breads have created a new niche for gourmet sandwiches. Restaurant chefs are assembling their bread baskets with greater care, choosing loaves that will complement the tastes and textures of individual courses. Rustic artisan breads are finding new uses in breakfast, lunch, and dinner, lending a complexity to casseroles, lasagnas, and even desserts that grocery-shelf slices could never match.

We define artisan, or artisanal, bread as handcrafted, European-style loaves that are created by a skilled baker using fresh ingredients and baked in a stone deck oven. Traditionally, artisan breads have a crisp, deeply hued crust and moist, chewy crumb, or middle. They are chemical and preservative free and crafted from the highest-quality all natural ingredients. All artisan breads start with flour, water, salt, and a natural leavening agent, like yeast. The skill of the baker transforms these simple ingredients into the incredible variety of artisan loaves we offer to customers in communities across the nation.

When most of us think of bread, we think of something that is basic but nonetheless special. Artisan bread is perhaps even more exceptional. At Panera Bread we take great pride in creating a sense of connectivity that people are missing in today's busy world. We do this with each loaf we bake. Made with our unique starter, our breads are individually hand-shaped and hand-scored and come in an array of shapes and flavors—with tangy cheeses, piquant Greek olives, or rich pecans. At Panera Bread, we are bringing the taste of old-world tradition to new communities and neighborhoods every day.

There is a reason why nearly every culture comes together to "break bread" as friends and family members. At Panera, we understand that the universal spirit of bread is sharing. And learning more about bread and bread baking allows us to connect with each other in new, meaningful ways.

Great breads share hallmark characteristics in color, shape, aroma, taste, and texture. Here are some things to look for when judging a loaf of handcrafted bread:

- A finely crafted loaf should be symmetrical and evenly shaped. As you look at the exterior of the bread, the thickness and color of the crust should be consistent around the circumference of the loaf.

- Scores, or cuts, along the top of the loaf are a hallmark of artisan breads. Scores allow for gases and steam to escape from breads while baking and help to ensure an evenly baked loaf. The scores should have a lighter appearance than the rest of the crust.

- Take some time to look inside at the crumb of the loaf. The cell structure of the crumb should be open and consistent from end to end. An open cell structure is defined by midsized to large holes throughout the crumb and allows for better and more complex flavor than the small-crumbed, mass-produced breads that are commonly found on supermarket shelves. The air pockets indicate proper handling of the dough throughout the fermentation and baking process.

- Listen to your bread. Survey the loaf by gently tapping on the bottom with your knuckles and listening for a low, soft sound, indicating a thorough bake. As you break open the loaf, there should be a hearty crackling sound from the crispness of the crust. Some breads, such as French bread, will make a cacophony of crackling noises without any provocation when they are fresh out of the oven and set out to cool as gases escape and pressure changes occur.

- There are also many things that can be learned from the aroma of a particular bread. Walk into any Panera Bread bakery-cafe and the smell of fresh bread is immediately apparent. The nutlike fragrance of the flour and the slightly sour scent of artisan leaven combine to make a uniquely pleasant, mild aroma. Break open a loaf and smell the crumb as you would a fine wine before tasting. Inhale the hints of the various spices and natural ingredients that provide the complexity and flavor of the bread.

Having helped nurture the shift toward artisan breads, we wrote this cookbook to share our knowledge and passion for bread with our customers and with home cooks across the country. Bread lovers will find a wide selection of traditional dishes, new variations on family favorites, and unique combinations that perfectly pair the ingredients with the characteristics of individual artisan loaves.

To get you started, our trained artisan bakers have developed easy-to-follow bread formulas and techniques for baking at home with the tools and equipment found in the standard kitchen. This cookbook focuses on fundamentals, providing simple instructions that are guaranteed to create the perfect loaf in less than three hours. Home bakers interested in furthering their knowledge and skills also will find here an explanation of the science of baking and a few advanced techniques. Great bread takes time and practice, and in that process of trial and error we believe you will find that the true joy of baking bread for and with loved ones is in the experience as much as the final product.

We hope that the recipes and information in this book will help bring people back into the kitchen, and continue a baking tradition that has united families and friends for thousands of years.

PANERA BREAD MENU FAVORITES

Throughout this cookbook, several recipes are noted with this special icon:

Panera is proud to share recipes from its award-winning bakery-cafe menu with readers of *The Panera Bread Cookbook*. The featured dishes celebrate the winning combination of fresh produce, high quality meats and cheeses, flavorful sauces and dressings, and, of course, freshly baked artisan bread.

[PART ONE]

Bread Baking 101:
Building Your Knowledge of Bread

In this section we explore the basics of breadmaking, working with simple recipes for handcrafted bread. At Panera Bread, we use bread formulas that require several days of fermentation to achieve the complex flavors and characteristics of our signature loaves. However, recognizing that most people have far less time when baking at home, we have created modified formulas to allow home bakers to craft a quality loaf of bread from scratch in just three hours. Don't be intimidated by the idea of baking bread at home. Great handcrafted breads begin with just a few simple ingredients combined with some basic techniques.

Once you've mastered the basics, we hope that you will experiment on your own, adding and adjusting ingredients to create your own extraordinary works of edible art. At the end of this section you'll find a formula for a natural sourdough starter, and three additional bread recipes that use this starter to lend unique characteristics to the breads. These recipes are provided to help you understand how small variations in ingredients and technique can significantly change the final taste and texture of your homemade loaves.

Learning to Bake
with Formulas

When most of us enter the kitchen to prepare a meal, we use a
recipe as our culinary guide. Substituting ingredients or adjusting the
measurements may have little effect on the final dish. Bread baking,
however, relies on precise chemical reactions, which are greatly
affected by the slightest alteration of environment. To understand
this chemistry, you must first understand the ingredients.

All true artisan breads start with four simple ingredients.

Leavening Agent

The leavening agent, typically the microscopic organism yeast, feeds off of the sugars in hydrated flour, producing as a by-product alcohol and carbon dioxide gas. This process, called fermentation, provides flavor and gives structure to the loaf.

The three most common varieties of yeast available for the home baker are fresh, instant, and active dry yeasts. All of the recipes in this cookbook call for fresh yeast. We prefer to use fresh yeast because it lends a deeper flavor than dried and instant varieties while providing a strong rise to the dough. However, in some markets fresh yeast can be difficult to find, so you can easily substitute instant or active dry yeast. When converting from fresh yeast, the standard ratio is one-half (50 percent) as much active dry yeast and one-third (33 percent) as much instant yeast.

Flour

Flour, when hydrated, releases sugars for the yeast to feed on and when kneaded, creates the gluten needed to form what is known as the protein matrix. This matrix, which gives dough a sticky texture, acts like a balloon, trapping the carbon dioxide gas produced by the yeast and giving the loaf its shape.

The recipes in this cookbook can be made with any commercially available variety of flour. You will notice that the type of flour used in the creation of the starter will determine the variety of bread you will make. Wheat flour in the starter will create a wheat loaf, corn flour in the starter will create a corn bread, and rye flour in the starter will result in a rye bread. All-purpose flour in the starter will produce a standard white loaf.

Flour is classified by the type of grain it is produced from and the amount of gluten it has. During the mixing process, gluten forms the structure for the bread, therefore the higher its gluten content, the better the flour will be for baking bread. Rye and soy flours have low levels of gluten, and therefore cannot be used alone, but must be used in combination with other flours for breadmaking. Wheat flour contains high levels of gluten, and is therefore the flour of choice for bread.

There are various types of wheat flour, classified by their amount of gluten. Cake and pastry flours range from 6 to 10 percent gluten. On average, all-purpose flour has 10 percent gluten. Bread flour, which is made from hard winter wheat, has around 12 to 13 percent gluten. All-purpose flour to which the manufacturer has added salt and a leavening agent is called self-rising flour.

Water

Water hydrates the flour, enabling the development of gluten and the protein matrix when mixed or kneaded. Warm water (95–105°F.) helps activate the yeast and initiate fermentation, the process of yeast feeding on the sugars in the flour and releasing carbon dioxide and alcohol. Bottled or filtered waters can be used in households with hard water.

Salt

Salt is used to enhance the flavor and help control the rate of fermentation. Without salt, the yeast would feed too quickly on the sugars in the flour, exhausting its food source and dying before it fully leavens the bread.

Additional Ingredients

Many Panera formulas call for hours, and others for days, of fermentation to develop the complex flavors and textures in our signature loaves. The recreational baker has much less time, so the bread recipes in this cookbook incorporate honey and shortening. The honey provides additional sugars for the yeast to feed on, which speeds up fermentation. The shortening provides moisture and gives texture to the bread. Equal measurements of butter or olive oil may be substituted for shortening.

Controlling fermentation is the key to making great bread. Ingredient temperature, salt content, and time are all factors in fermentation.

Yeast moves and feeds more slowly as the temperature drops, and accelerates as the temperature increases. If the yeast feeds too quickly, it will exhaust its supply of sugars and starve to death, preventing it from providing the necessary lift to the dough. If it feeds too slowly, it will not provide the necessary flavor to the dough. And high levels of salinity can halt fermentation by killing the yeast completely.

The ideal temperature for fermentation is 75–80°F. because it balances the time needed to produce great flavor and the time required to fully leaven the dough. At high altitudes, fermentation is accelerated due to a reduction in air pressure. Therefore, bakers in high altitudes often prefer to ferment in a cooler environment to slow down the rate of fermentation. Humidity often drops at higher altitudes as well, causing the flour to become drier and to absorb more liquid. Reducing the amount of flour or increasing the amount of liquid may be necessary to balance the formula at higher altitudes. As you become more skilled and experiment with advanced bread recipes, you will recognize how the unique environmental factors in your kitchen may alter the final product and you will need to make the necessary changes to the formulas.

With all these factors, bakers must use formulas, or recipes with fixed proportions, to help control these chemical reactions. Following formulas precisely, from measurement to temperature to time, will result in consistently good-quality bread every time you bake at home.

Baker's Percentages

When creating a formula, bakers use baker's percentages, which list ingredients by weight as a ratio of the overall weight of flour in the dough. This system of measurement is the most accurate way to adjust formulas, allowing you to re-create the correct balance of ingredients no matter how large or small the batch. All you need to know are the percentages and the amount of flour you will use.

Flour has a baker's percentage of 100 percent. To find baker's percentages when you have ingredient weights, simply divide the ingredient weight by the flour weight in the dough. In this example, we have divided each ingredient by the weight of flour (300 ounces for 20 loaves), giving us the baker's percentages of the water (65 percent), salt (2 percent), and yeast (2 percent).

```
Flour    300 ounces ÷ 300 = 100%
Water    195 ounces ÷ 300 = 65%
 Salt    6 ounces ÷ 300 = 2%
Yeast    6 ounces ÷ 300 = 2%
```

With these baker's percentages, we can then adjust the size of the batch accurately by multiplying our new flour weight (15 ounces for one loaf) by the baker's percentages of the other ingredients to get the new measurements needed for the adjusted formula for a smaller batch.

```
Adjusted flour weight    15 ounces
    Adjusted water    15 ounces x 65% = 9¾ ounces
            salt    15 ounces x 2% = ⅓ ounce
           yeast    15 ounces x 2% = ⅓ ounce
```

THE FORMULA:
Six Steps to Success

The formula for each of the breads in this cookbook is fundamentally the same. The only significant changes will be in the type of flour used and any additional ingredients, such as olives or onions. Otherwise, the percentages and the processes all follow the same basic six steps.

Step One: MAKING THE STARTER

A starter, also called a preferment, is a mixture of flour, water, and yeast that is allowed to ferment. The role of the starter is to extend the fermentation process, adding a depth of flavor and leavening strength to the dough. Were we to mix the dough without the starter, it would not rise as well, nor would it have the character and flavor of dough created with a starter.

For our beginner breads, we will be using a single-use starter with a batter-like consistency. This type of starter is known as a *poolish* and works very well in today's busy kitchen because the wetter consistency gives the yeast greater mobility, resulting in faster fermentation. This allows us to create the maximum amount of flavor in a short amount of time. At the end of the "Basic Bread Formulas" chapter, you will find a formula for a sourdough starter that can be refrigerated, replenished, and reused over an extended period of time to create consistent results in every batch of bread. Panera Bread's award-winning sourdough is created with a perpetual starter that is over twenty-five years old, and our bakers feed and use this "mother" in our bakery-cafes to create the same quality handcrafted breads in every Panera Bread across the country.

To make the single-use starter, dissolve the yeast in warm (95–105°F.) water until fully incorporated. Add the flour and whisk until smooth. Cover the container with a towel and allow the starter to ferment for 30 minutes.

Time is important when creating a starter. Allowing a starter to ferment longer than the formula designates will result in the yeast exhausting its food source and starving before it can serve as a leavening agent in the dough. Limiting fermentation to less time than designated in the formula will reduce the depth of flavor and leavening strength of the starter. For our standard bread formulas, be sure to ferment the starter for a half hour before mixing it with the other ingredients to form the dough.

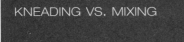

KNEADING VS. MIXING

While kneading dough can be an enjoyable step in breadmaking, an electric mixer with a dough hook saves both time and effort. A mixer is especially useful when working with wet or sticky dough. A number of models are available at most kitchen and home supply stores.

Step Two: MIXING THE DOUGH

Mixing the dough is the most critical step in the creation of gluten, the protein responsible for creating the size and shape of a loaf of bread. When flour is hydrated and mixed, simple proteins in the flour bond together to form gluten, a protein that forms a matrix in the dough that will trap the carbon dioxide produced by the yeast during fermentation. The creation of gluten in dough through mixing or kneading is called development. Without gluten, dough would not be able to rise or hold its shape when baked in the oven.

As dough develops, it becomes smooth and less sticky. Developed dough is elastic and capable of being formed into loaves. Undermixed dough will not fully form the protein matrix, and overmixing the dough will break down the matrix that was formed during development.

Mixer speed and dough temperature can affect the time needed for the dough to reach full development. Therefore, *recognizing the characteristics of fully-developed dough is more important than timing the process.* As the dough develops, it will begin pulling away from the sides of the mixing bowl. This is the first sign of development. Once the dough pulls away from the sides and begins "cleaning" the sides of the bowl, stop the mixer. Take a small piece of dough from the mixer and stretch it slowly

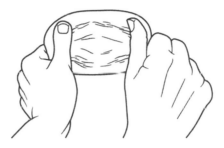

between your fingers. If the dough tears easily, continue mixing for a minute or two and retest. When the dough forms a translucent membrane, or "gluten window," when stretched, it is fully developed.

Step Three: RESTING

Once the dough has been fully developed in the mixer, it must rest. Resting the dough after development allows the gluten to relax, which will prevent the tearing of the dough when forming the loaves. During this step, the yeast will continue to feed on the sugars and multiply. This will cause the dough to become smooth and increase in size.

Step Four: SHAPING

There is an endless variety of shapes that can lend an artistic flair or useful form to your bread. Here's how to create five of the more common shapes:

THE BÂTARD OR PAN LOAF

This is a traditional, torpedo-shaped loaf. To create a bâtard, flatten the dough into a rectangle about 1 inch thick. Begin folding the top edge down toward you, pinching the seam closed as you go. When you have folded the loaf to the bottom edge, pinch the seam to seal. Pinch each end closed, fold under, and set the loaf aside on a surface lightly sprinkled with cornmeal (which will prevent the dough from sticking), or place in a greased loaf pan. Always make sure the seams are sealed tightly and folded under the bottom of the loaf to prevent them from reopening as the bread expands in the oven.

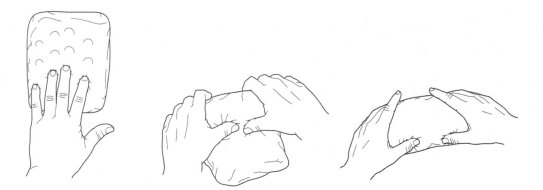

THE BAGUETTE

Fold the dough into a bâtard loaf using the method above. Once formed, carefully roll the loaf with the palms of your hands, pressing down and out until the loaf is the desired width and length. Set the loaf aside on a surface lightly sprinkled with cornmeal.

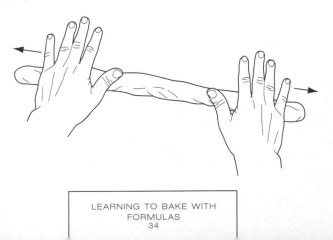

THE BOULE

This popular round loaf is great for creating edible containers for dips and soups. Start with a round ball of dough. Create tension in the dough by pinching the outsides of the ball of dough together. The dough will begin to tighten as your fingers move closer to the center of the ball of dough. Tightly seal the seam you have created. Finish by placing the boule seam-side down on the counter and rotate it carefully between your hands to create a smooth, round shape. Set aside on a surface that has been lightly sprinkled with cornmeal.

THE BRAID

Form three baguette loaves of even length and size. Pinch the three loaves together at one end. Carefully braid the right strand of dough over the middle strand; then alternating from left to right, braid the outside strands over the middle strand until you reach the bottom. Pinch the three ends together and set the loaf aside on a surface lightly sprinkled with cornmeal.

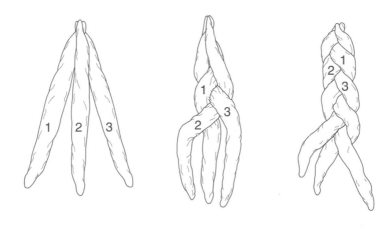

To create a bagel, take a ball of dough about the size of your fist and press your finger through the center, pushing it all the way through the dough. Carefully expand the center of the hole as desired and set aside on a surface lightly sprinkled with cornmeal.

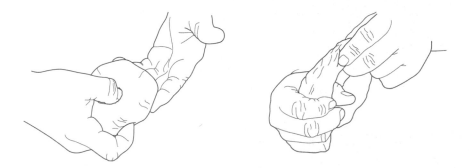

Step Five: PROOFING AND SCORING

PROOFING

Proofing dough is much like resting dough. During the shaping of the loaf, the gas that was trapped in the protein matrix escapes, and the dough loses much of its size. Proofing is simply setting the loaf aside after shaping to allow the yeast to replenish the carbon dioxide that provides the shape and size of a loaf of bread.

Set the dough aside and cover with a warm, moist cloth. This will prevent the loaves from forming a skin that stops the loaf from rising fully in the oven. If you plan to bake your bread in a loaf pan, proof the dough in the pan, spraying it first with cooking spray to prevent it from sticking. Many bakers place their loaves to proof on top of a warm oven. The warmth from the oven speeds up fermentation, creating more carbon dioxide and causing the dough to rise more quickly.

After proofing, handle the dough carefully so that additional carbon dioxide does not escape. One way to test if the loaf has proofed properly is to press the loaf gently with a finger. If the indentation remains, the loaf is proofed and ready to bake. In our standard bread formulas, a proof time of 30 minutes is all that is needed.

SCORING

Centuries ago, families baked in community ovens and would score their loaves in a distinctive way to differentiate their bread from that of the other families. This tradition continues today in bakeries across the world, with many bakers branding their loaves with a signature score.

Scoring also is functional. While baking, the temperature of the loaf increases quickly. Activated by heat, the yeast feeds more rapidly on the sugars in the dough, creating more carbon dioxide and causing the loaf to rise rapidly, or "bloom."

The expanding gas will find the weakest point in the surface of the loaf to escape. Scores in the surface of the bread give the carbon dioxide a designated vent. If the bread is not scored, the sides of the loaf often will burst, giving the bread an irregular shape and appearance.

A thin, sharp edge is best for scoring loaves before putting them in the oven. Many bakers prefer a razor blade or baker's lame, but a paring knife or small chef's knife works equally well. Scores should be fairly deep—about one-half inch deep for a small boule to one inch deep for a standard loaf—and at a slight angle. Angled scores will create an attractive "lip" when baked. Three scores are enough for a standard loaf of bread, but more may be appropriate for larger loaves, such as baguettes. Avoid overscoring, which can damage the protein matrix of the bread and prevent a full rise in the oven.

Step Six: BAKING

Once the bread is proofed and scored, it is ready to be baked. The oven and baking stone (if using) should be preheated to 400°F. for at least an hour before baking. Lightly spray the loaf of bread with water and place in the oven. If baking in a loaf pan, place it directly on the rack. If not using a loaf pan, the bread should be baked directly on the baking stone. Spraying the loaf with water accomplishes several things. First, it will prevent the crust from forming until the loaf has risen fully, guaranteeing a fully formed loaf of bread. Second, it introduces steam into the baking process, aiding in the conduction of heat and adding moisture to the bread.

The heat from the oven causes a reaction between the carbohydrates and proteins in the dough. This process, called the Maillard reaction, is responsible for the flavor, color, texture, and aroma of the bread. The high temperature also caramelizes the sugars in the dough, lending a deep brown hue to the crust. As the temperature of the baking bread increases, the yeast eventually dies, preventing the dough from rising further. At about 160°F, the starches in the bread become more rigid, setting the form of the loaf.

Baking times will vary by oven, but approximately 30 minutes is recommended for the recipes in this cookbook (bearing in mind that larger loaves will take longer to bake and smaller loaves will bake more quickly). Resist the urge to open the oven door when checking on the bread. Opening the oven releases hot air and rapidly cools the oven. When cooked through, artisan breads produce a hollow thump when tapped; however the best way to check for doneness is to use a thermometer. Insert the thermometer through the bottom of the loaf until it has reached the center. When the center of the bread is 190–200°F, the bread is ready to come out of the oven.

Allow freshly baked breads to cool for at least 30 minutes before slicing. This allows some of the excess moisture within the loaf to evaporate, and gives the crumb, or center of the bread, time to set. Cooling bread on your countertop or kitchen table can result in a soggy crust; therefore, we recommend cooling loaves on a baker's rack to help circulate the air around the entire loaf of bread. If you do not have a baker's rack, you may remove a rack from your oven before preheating and set it aside to cool your bread on after baking.

Storing Bread

Artisan bread is best enjoyed within 48 hours of baking. However, there are a number of ways to extend its shelf life for days and even weeks. Panera's master artisan baker recommends storing unused loaves at room temperature in a bread box or sealed paper bag for up to three days. Sliced loaves should be stored cut side down to limit the crumb's exposure to air.

Avoid storing room temperature loaves in plastic bags, which will soften the crust by trapping moisture, creating a good environment for mold to grow. Storing breads in the refrigerator speeds up the staling process and should be avoided unless the bread contains meats and other perishable ingredients.

Frozen loaves can be thawed and enjoyed for 2 to 3 weeks after baking. Wrap fully cooled loaves in foil or plastic wrap, seal in a plastic bag, and store in the freezer. Thaw frozen loaves in the plastic bag for 2 to 3 hours, remove the foil or plastic wrap, and bake for 5 to 10 minutes in a 400°F. oven to restore a crisp crust.

Organizing the Baker's Kitchen

People have been baking bread for thousands of years with the most basic of tools. As technology has advanced, so has our ability to create great bread simply and efficiently in our homes. Electric mixers, digital scales, and a variety of other useful tools, while not mandatory for baking, make it easier to consistently make high quality artisan loaves in the standard kitchen. We believe that the easier it is to craft great bread at home, the more likely it is you will make homemade breads part of your family table. In this section we have included an overview of the equipment and tools we suggest for the beginning home baker.

Stand Mixer with Dough Hook

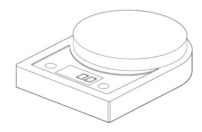

The formulas in this cookbook were created specifically for use with a heavy-duty electric mixer. All of the recipes can be created through hand-kneading, but for simplicity and speed we recommend an electric mixer fitted with a dough hook. Viking and KitchenAid offer a variety of quality models.

Digital Scale

A digital scale is a good investment for the home baker. Bread recipes involve chemical reactions that must be controlled by using a precise ratio of ingredients. Digital scales are available at most kitchen and home supply stores.

Pizza Stone or Removable Stone Deck

While not essential to baking great bread at home, baking on a stone is the best way to create the crisp, deeply hued crust that is the hallmark of artisan breads. Baking on a stone facilitates caramelization of the sugars

in the dough and draws moisture from the crust. Stone retains and radiates heat more effectively than metal, providing a steady, even heat for baking. All of the breads in this cookbook can be baked in a standard loaf pan, but we recommend purchasing a stone deck or inexpensive pizza stone for your oven. Baking stones are available at most kitchen and home supply stores.

Quality Mixing Bowls

Many bakers prefer to use ceramic or wood bowls rather than metal or glass. These porous materials provide a good home for yeast, which can live indefinitely in a "seasoned" bowl, giving more rise and strength to future batches of dough. To sustain the yeast cultures in a mixing bowl, rinse with warm water and wipe clean with a dry cloth after each use. Do not use soap, which can kill yeast.

Lame or Paring Knife

Many bakers prefer to use a razor or traditional baker's lame, but any small, sharp knife will work for scoring loaves.

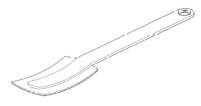

Clean Cloths

We recommend having several clean cloths on hand when making bread. Covering the mixing bowl while the starter is fermenting will help the starter retain heat. Covering the loaves with a warm, moist cloth will prevent the dough from forming a premature crust, which will limit its ability to rise in the oven.

Instant-Read Kitchen Thermometer

Beginning bakers often are encouraged to maintain strict control of the temperature of their ingredients, the environment, and the dough through every stage of breadmaking. However, this practice can be intimidating to new bakers who are just starting out, preventing them from experimenting with bread at home. The beginner bread recipes in this cookbook have been developed to forgive small variations in temperature and measurement, and we suggest you try these once through without keeping strict control of temperatures. As a rule of thumb, the ideal temperature of the dough and the surrounding environment is 75–80°F. Temperatures below 75°F. will retard the yeast in the dough; temperatures above 80°F. will speed the yeast up. Keeping the dough within this temperature range will produce the best results, and as you become more skilled and experiment with advanced bread recipes, you will recognize how the temperature of the dough and your environment can affect the final product.

Loaf Pans

Loaf pans provide a traditional shape that is ideal for sandwiches. A standard 8½ × 4½ × 2½-inch loaf pan can be found at most local grocers and at kitchen and home supply stores. When choosing a loaf pan, it is important to consider how different characteristics of the pan will affect the final loaf of bread. Aluminum conducts heat better than stainless steel, making it a better choice if using a metal pan. Dark-colored materials retain and conduct heat better than light materials, 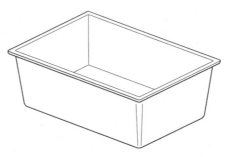 speeding up baking times. Glass or ceramic pans radiate heat steadily and evenly throughout the baking process. This makes them a good choice when baking in older, less efficient ovens.

Spray Bottle

Artisan bakers have a number of methods for introducing steam to the baking process. At Panera Bread, we use steam-injection ovens to provide the moisture needed to allow the breads to rise fully in the oven and create a crispy, golden crust. Home bakers can spray loaves with water before placing them in the oven to achieve a similar effect.

Dough Knife (Bench Scraper)

This tool is commonly used by bakers to cut and manipulate dough. It can be purchased at most kitchen and home supply stores.

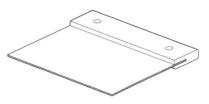

Bannetons

Proofing baskets come in a variety of shapes and sizes, but the French banneton is the most popular. Bread proofed in a banneton retains the distinct patterns of the basket, adding a unique and attractive design to the loaf. Bannetons can be purchased at select kitchen and home supply stores.

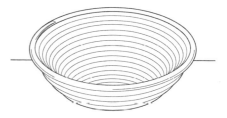

Basic Bread Formulas:
The Recipes

The following formulas can be used to craft high-quality loaves of bread in only three hours, using the equipment that can be found in a standard home kitchen. We recommend that you read Learning to Bake with Formulas (pages 27–43) before diving into the formulas. Doing so will provide you with a list of equipment you will need to bake these breads and additional information to help you troubleshoot problems along the way.

The formulas are broken down into white, wheat, and rye varieties, starting with a plain recipe for each and then offering a few versions that incorporate fresh herbs, fruits, and other ingredients. You will notice that the type of flour used in the creation of the starter is what determines the variety of bread you will end up making. Keep this in mind as you work through these formulas. Once you have successfully baked these basic breads, try experimenting with other varieties of flour in the starter to add different textures and flavors.

In addition to the basic bread formulas, we have included a formula for a sourdough starter and three additional bread recipes that use this multi-use, or perpetual, starter. As you become more comfortable with these basic formulas, we encourage you to experiment with the advanced formulas and eventually try creating new formulas with your favorite ingredients and techniques.

There are a few important tips you should keep in mind before baking your first artisan bread with our basic formulas:

- Read the formula all the way through before beginning; verify that you have all of the ingredients you will need and the time to complete the entire formula.

- Follow the formula exactly as it is listed in the cookbook at least one time through before experimenting. Inexperienced bakers will sometimes make small changes to a formula on their first attempt and become frustrated when the bread does not turn out well. Follow the formulas as they are listed until you successfully create a loaf of great bread, and then feel free to experiment with new ingredients and techniques.

- If you are using a digital scale, check to make sure it is in good working order before measuring ingredients. A scale resetting in the middle of weighing ingredients could lead to incorrect measurements.

- Test your oven. With an oven thermometer, measure the cycles of your oven before baking. If it runs hot or cold, calibrate your oven per the manufacturer's instructions.

- When using a formula, it is necessary to combine the ingredients in the exact order listed. Although changing the order may not seem significant, incorporation in the correct order is required to achieve an exact replication of the formula.

- Always measure dry ingredients before adding them to liquid ingredients. That way, if you make a mistake while measuring, you can remove some of the dry ingredient before it is dissolved in the liquid.

- Never put salt directly on yeast. Doing so will kill the yeast, and your bread will not rise properly.

- For accuracy, bakers weigh their ingredients rather than measuring them by volume; it is the most precise method for guaranteeing the correct baker's percentage. A cup of sifted flour is noticeably less than a cup of unsifted flour when measured by volume. However, when measured by weight, a pound of sifted flour is equal to a pound of unsifted flour. Weighing ingredients prevents inconsistencies that can occur in baking when measuring by volume. Of course we understand that volume measurements may make our formulas more acessible to the average home baker, so we have provided ingredient amounts in both volume and weight. If you own a kitchen scale, we recommend following the weight measurements to ensure the most reliable results.

Country White Bread

STARTER

1   cup (8.375 ounces) warm water (95–105°F.)
2   teaspoons (.25 ounce) fresh yeast
1   cup (4.875 ounces) all-purpose flour

DOUGH

¾   cup (5.75 ounces) warm water (95–105°F.)
3   tablespoons (2 ounces) honey
4   teaspoons (.5 ounce) fresh yeast
¼   cup + 1 teaspoon (2 ounces) vegetable shortening
4¾ cups (22 ounces) all-purpose flour
1   tablespoon (.5 ounce) salt
    Starter

TO CREATE THE STARTER, combine the water and yeast in a medium mixing bowl. Stir to dissolve the yeast fully. Add the flour to the bowl and stir until the ingredients are fully incorporated. Cover with a cloth and ferment the starter at room temperature for 30 minutes.

FOR THE DOUGH, combine the water, honey, and yeast in the bowl of a stand mixer. Stir to dissolve the yeast fully. Add the shortening, flour, salt, and fermented starter. Mix on low speed until the dough is fully developed. Remove the dough from the mixing bowl.

Divide the dough into 2 pieces weighing about 22 ounces each. Set aside any remaining dough and freeze for future use. Roll each piece of dough into a smooth ball. Place the dough on the counter or in a proofing basket and cover with a warm, damp cloth to rest at room temperature for 30 minutes. Preheat the oven to 400°F.

Form the dough into loaves, cover with a warm, damp cloth, and proof at room temperature for 30 minutes.

Score the loaves with a sharp knife, spray with water, and bake for 30 to 40 minutes, or until the crusts are a deep golden brown and the middle of the loaves is 190–200°F.

Remove the bread from the oven and place on a cooling rack for 30 minutes. If the bread was baked in loaf pans, remove the bread from the pans before cooling.

Cinnamon Raisin White Bread

MAKES 2 LOAVES

STARTER

1   cup (8.375 ounces) warm water (95–105°F.)
2   teaspoons (.25 ounce) fresh yeast
1   cup (4.875 ounces) all-purpose flour

DOUGH

¾   cup (5.75 ounces) warm water (95–105°F.)
3   tablespoons (2 ounces) honey
4   teaspoons (.5 ounce) fresh yeast
¼   cup + 1 teaspoon (2 ounces) vegetable shortening
4¾   cups (23 ounces) all-purpose flour
1   tablespoon (.5 ounce) salt
    Starter
1¼   cups (5.3 ounces) golden raisins
1   cup (5.3 ounces) cinnamon chips

TO CREATE THE STARTER, combine the water and yeast in a medium mixing bowl. Stir to dissolve the yeast fully. Add the flour to the bowl and stir until the ingredients are fully incorporated. Cover with a cloth and ferment the starter at room temperature for 30 minutes.

FOR THE DOUGH, combine the water, honey, and yeast in the bowl of a stand mixer. Stir to dissolve the yeast fully. Add the shortening, flour, salt, starter, and raisins. Mix the dough on low speed for 3 minutes. Add the cinnamon chips and mix on low speed until the dough is fully developed. Remove the dough from the mixing bowl.

Divide the dough into 2 pieces weighing about 22 ounces each. Set aside any remaining dough and freeze for future use. Roll each piece of dough into a smooth ball. Place the dough on the counter or in a proofing basket and cover with a warm, damp cloth to rest at room temperature for 30 minutes. Preheat the oven to 400°F.

Form the dough into loaves, cover with a warm, damp cloth, and proof at room temperature for 30 minutes.

Score the loaves with a sharp knife, spray with water, and bake for 30 to 40 minutes, until the crusts are a deep golden brown and the middle of the loaves is 190–200°F.

Remove the bread from the oven and place on a cooling rack for 30 minutes. If the bread was baked in loaf pans, remove the bread from the pans before cooling.

Raisin Pecan White Bread

Increase the warm water in the dough to 1¼ cups (10.469 ounces), reduce the raisins to 1 cup (5 ounces), and substitute 1 cup (5 ounces) of chopped pecans for the cinnamon chips.

Kalamata Olive Bread

MAKES 2 LOAVES

STARTER

1	cup (8.375 ounces) warm water (95–105°F.)
2	teaspoons (.25 ounce) fresh yeast
1	cup (4.875 ounces) all-purpose flour

DOUGH

⅔	cup (4.75 ounces) warm water (95–105°F.)
3	tablespoons (2 ounces) honey
4	teaspoons (.5 ounce) fresh yeast
¼	cup + 1 teaspoon (2 ounces) vegetable shortening
4¾	cups (23 ounces) all-purpose flour
1	tablespoon (.5 ounce) salt
	Starter
1¾	cups (8.5 ounces) kalamata olives, pitted

TO CREATE THE STARTER, combine the water and yeast in a medium mixing bowl. Stir to dissolve the yeast fully. Add the flour to the bowl and stir until the ingredients are fully incorporated. Cover with a cloth and ferment the starter at room temperature for 30 minutes.

FOR THE DOUGH, combine the water, honey, and yeast in the bowl of a stand mixer. Stir to dissolve the yeast fully. Add the shortening, flour, salt, starter, and olives. Mix on low speed until the dough is fully developed. Remove the dough from the mixing bowl. Divide the dough into 2 pieces weighing about 22 ounces each. Set aside any remaining dough and freeze for future use. Roll each piece of dough into a smooth ball. Place the dough on the counter or in a proofing basket and cover with a warm, damp cloth to rest at room temperature for 30 minutes. Preheat the oven to 400°F.

Form the dough into loaves and place them on the counter or in a proofing basket. Cover the loaves with a warm, damp cloth, and proof at room temperature for 30 minutes.

Score the loaves with a sharp knife, spray with water, and bake for 30 to 40 minutes, until the crusts are a deep golden brown and the middle of the loaves is 190–200°F.

Remove the bread from the oven and place on a cooling rack for 30 minutes. If the bread was baked in loaf pans, remove the bread from the pans before cooling.

Focaccia Bread

MAKES 2 PANS

2	cups (16 ounces) warm water (95–105°F.)
4	teaspoons (.5 ounce) fresh yeast
½	cup (3.67 ounces) extra-virgin olive oil
3	cups (14.625 ounces) all-purpose flour
1	cup (2 ounces) dried potato buds
2	teaspoons (.33 ounce) salt
1	tablespoon (.1 ounce) dried rosemary or basil (optional)

COMBINE THE WATER and yeast in the bowl of a stand mixer. Stir to dissolve the yeast fully. Add the oil, flour, potato buds, salt, and rosemary. Mix on low speed until all of the ingredients are incorporated and the dough becomes smooth in consistency (about 3 to 5 minutes). Pour half of the dough (it will be very wet) into a 9 × 6 × 1-inch aluminum foil pan sprayed with cooking spray. With your fingers, spread the dough out evenly in the pan, and brush the top with extra-virgin olive oil. Preheat the oven to 400°F. and, if possible, place the pan on top of the oven to proof for 1½ hours. (We recommend placing the aluminum foil pan on a baking sheet so that the pan is evenly heated while proofing.)

Bake for 25 minutes, or until the crust is a deep golden brown and the middle of the loaf is 190–200°F. Remove the bread from the oven and from the pan and place on a cooling rack for 30 minutes.

Three-Cheese Bread

STARTER

1   cup (8.375 ounces) warm water (95–105°F.)
2   teaspoons (.25 ounce) fresh yeast
1   cup (4.875 ounces) all-purpose flour

DOUGH

¾   cup (5.75 ounces) warm water (95–105°F.)
3   tablespoons (2 ounces) honey
4   teaspoons (.5 ounce) fresh yeast
¼   cup + 1 teaspoon (2 ounces) vegetable shortening
4¾   cups (23 ounces) all-purpose flour
1   tablespoon (.5 ounce) salt
½   cup (2 ounces) ½-inch cubes Romano cheese
½   cup (2 ounces) ½-inch cubes Parmesan cheese
½   cup (2 ounces) ½-inch cubes Asiago cheese
     Starter

TO CREATE THE STARTER, combine the water and yeast in a medium mixing bowl. Stir to dissolve the yeast fully. Add the flour to the bowl and stir until the ingredients are fully incorporated. Cover with a cloth and ferment the starter at room temperature for 30 minutes.

FOR THE DOUGH, combine the water, honey, and yeast in the bowl of a stand mixer. Stir to dissolve the yeast fully. Add the shortening, flour, salt, cheeses, and fermented starter. Mix on low speed until the dough is fully developed. Remove the dough from the mixing bowl.

Divide the dough into 2 pieces weighing about 22 ounces each. Set aside any remaining dough and freeze for future use. Roll each piece of dough into a smooth ball. Place the dough on the counter or in a proofing basket and cover with a warm, damp cloth to rest at room temperature for 30 minutes. Preheat the oven to 400°F.

Form the dough into loaves, cover with a warm, damp cloth, and proof at room temperature for 30 minutes.

Score the loaves with a sharp knife, spray with water, and bake for 30 minutes, or until the crusts are a deep golden brown and the middle of the loaves is 190–200°F.

Remove the bread from the oven and place on a cooling rack for 30 minutes. If the bread was baked in loaf pans, remove the bread from the pans before cooling.

Honey Wheat Bread

MAKES 2 LOAVES

STARTER

1	cup (8.375 ounces) warm water (95–105°F.)	
2	teaspoons (.25 ounce) fresh yeast	
1	cup (4.875 ounces) whole-wheat flour	

DOUGH

¾	cup (5.75 ounces) warm water (95–105°F.)	
3	tablespoons (2 ounces) honey	
4	teaspoons (.5 ounce) fresh yeast	
¼	cup + 1 teaspoon (2 ounces) vegetable shortening	
4¾	cups (23 ounces) all-purpose flour	
1	tablespoon (.5 ounce) salt	
	Starter	

TO CREATE THE STARTER, combine the water and yeast in a medium mixing bowl. Stir to dissolve the yeast fully. Add the flour to the bowl and stir until the ingredients are fully incorporated. Cover with a cloth and ferment the starter at room temperature for 30 minutes.

FOR THE DOUGH, combine the water, honey, and yeast in the bowl of a stand mixer. Stir to dissolve the yeast fully. Add the shortening, flour, salt, and starter. Mix on low speed until the dough is fully developed. Remove the dough from the mixing bowl.

Divide the dough into 2 pieces weighing about 22 ounces each. Set aside any remaining dough and freeze for future use. Roll each piece of dough into a smooth ball. Place the dough on the counter or in a proofing basket and cover with a warm, damp cloth to rest at room temperature for 30 minutes. Preheat the oven to 400°F.

Form the dough into loaves, cover with a warm, damp cloth, and proof at room temperature for 30 minutes.

Score the loaves with a sharp knife, spray with water, and bake for 30 to 40 minutes, or until the crusts are a deep golden brown and the middle of the loaves is 190–200°F.

Remove the bread from the oven and place on a cooling rack for 30 minutes. If the bread was baked in loaf pans, remove the bread from the pans before cooling.

Garlic Olive Wheat Bread

MAKES 2 LOAVES

STARTER

1	cup (8.375 ounces) warm water (95–105°F.)
2	teaspoons (.25 ounce) fresh yeast
1	cup (4.875 ounces) whole-wheat flour

DOUGH

⅔	cup (4.725 ounces) warm water (95–105°F.)
3	tablespoons (2 ounces) honey
4	teaspoons (.5 ounce) fresh yeast
¼	cup + 1 teaspoon (2 ounces) vegetable shortening
4¾	cups (23 ounces) all-purpose flour
1	tablespoon (.5 ounce) salt
	Starter
1¾	cups (8.5 ounces) garlic stuffed olives

TO CREATE THE STARTER, combine the water and yeast in a medium mixing bowl. Stir to dissolve the yeast fully. Add the flour to the bowl and stir until the ingredients are fully incorporated. Cover with a cloth and ferment the starter at room temperature for 30 minutes.

FOR THE DOUGH, combine the water, honey, and yeast in the bowl of a stand mixer. Stir to dissolve the yeast fully. Add the shortening, flour, salt, starter, and olives. Mix on low speed until the dough is fully developed. Remove the dough from the mixing bowl.

Divide the dough into 2 pieces weighing about 22 ounces each. Set aside any remaining dough and freeze for future use. Roll each piece of dough into a smooth ball. Place the dough on the counter or in a proofing basket and cover with a warm, damp cloth to rest at room temperature for 30 minutes. Preheat the oven to 400°F.

Form the dough into loaves, cover with a warm, damp cloth, and proof at room temperature for 30 minutes.

Score the loaves with a sharp knife, spray with water, and bake for 30 to 40 minutes, or until the crusts are a deep golden brown and the middle of the loaves is 190–200°F.

Remove the bread from the oven and place on a cooling rack for 30 minutes. If the bread was baked in loaf pans, remove the bread from the pans before cooling.

Vegetable Wheat Bread

MAKES 2 LOAVES

STARTER

1	cup (8.375 ounces) warm water (95–105°F.)
2	teaspoons (.25 ounce) fresh yeast
1	cup (4.875 ounces) whole-wheat flour

DOUGH

¾	cup (5.75 ounces) warm water (95–105°F.)
3	tablespoons (2 ounces) honey
4	teaspoons (.5 ounce) fresh yeast
¼	cup + 1 teaspoon (2 ounces) vegetable shortening
4¾	cups (23 ounces) all-purpose flour
1	tablespoon (.5 ounce) salt
	Starter
¾	cup (7.75 ounces) dried vegetable soup mix

TO CREATE THE STARTER, combine the water and yeast in a medium
mixing bowl. Stir to dissolve the yeast fully. Add the flour to the bowl
and stir until the ingredients are fully incorporated. Cover with a cloth
and ferment the starter at room temperature for 30 minutes.

FOR THE DOUGH, combine the water, honey, and yeast in the bowl of a
stand mixer. Stir to dissolve the yeast fully. Add the shortening, flour, salt,
starter, and vegetable soup mix. Mix on low speed until the dough is
fully developed. Remove the dough from the mixing bowl.

Divide the dough into 2 pieces weighing about 22 ounces each. Set aside
any remaining dough and freeze for future use. Roll each piece of dough
into a smooth ball. Place the dough on the counter or in a proofing
basket and cover with a warm, damp cloth to rest at room temperature
for 30 minutes. Preheat the oven to 400°F.

Form the dough into loaves, cover with a warm, damp cloth, and proof at room temperature for 30 minutes.

Score the loaves with a sharp knife, spray with water, and bake for 30 to 40 minutes, or until the crusts are a deep golden brown and the middle of the loaves is 190–200°F.

Remove the bread from the oven and place on a cooling rack for 30 minutes. If the bread was baked in loaf pans, remove the bread from the pans before cooling.

Wheat Bread with Bacon and Onion

MAKES 2 LOAVES

STARTER

1	cup (8.375 ounces) warm water (95–105°F.)
2	teaspoons (.25 ounce) fresh yeast
1	cup (4.875 ounces) whole-wheat flour

DOUGH

¾	cup (5.75 ounces) warm water (95–105°F.)
3	tablespoons (2 ounces) honey
4	teaspoons (.5 ounce) fresh yeast
¼	cup + 1 teaspoon (2 ounces) vegetable shortening
4¾	cups (23 ounces) all-purpose flour
1	tablespoon (.5 ounce) salt
	Starter
1	cup (3.25 ounces) real bacon bits
2	tablespoons (.5 ounce) dehydrated onion

TO CREATE THE STARTER, combine the water and the yeast in a medium mixing bowl. Stir to dissolve the yeast fully. Add the flour to the bowl and stir until the ingredients are fully incorporated. Cover with a cloth and ferment the starter at room temperature for 30 minutes.

FOR THE DOUGH, combine the water, honey, and yeast in the bowl of a stand mixer. Stir to dissolve the yeast fully. Add the shortening, flour, salt, starter, bacon, and onion. Mix on low speed until the dough is fully developed. Remove the dough from the mixing bowl.

Divide the dough into 2 pieces weighing about 22 ounces each. Set aside any remaining dough and freeze for future use. Roll each piece of dough into a smooth ball. Place the dough on the counter or in a proofing basket and cover with a warm, damp cloth to rest at room temperature for 30 minutes. Preheat the oven to 400°F.

Form the dough into loaves, cover with a warm, damp cloth, and proof at room temperature for 30 minutes.

Score the loaves with a sharp knife, spray with water, and bake for 30 to 40 minutes, or until the crusts are a deep golden brown and the middle of the loaves is 190–200°F.

Remove the bread from the oven and place on a cooling rack for 30 minutes. If the bread was baked in loaf pans, remove the bread from the pans before cooling.

Rye Bread

MAKES 2 LOAVES

STARTER

1	cup (8.375 ounces) warm water (95–105°F.)
2	teaspoons (.25 ounce) fresh yeast
1	cup (4.875 ounces) dark rye flour

DOUGH

¾	cup (5.75 ounces) warm water (95–105°F.)
3	tablespoons (2 ounces) honey
4	teaspoons (.5 ounce) fresh yeast
¼	cup + 1 teaspoon (2 ounces) vegetable shortening
4¾	cups (23 ounces) all-purpose flour
1	tablespoon (.5 ounce) salt
	Starter
½	cup (1.75 ounces) dehydrated onion

TO CREATE THE STARTER, combine the water and yeast in a medium mixing bowl. Stir to dissolve the yeast fully. Add the flour to the bowl and stir until the ingredients are fully incorporated. Cover with a cloth and ferment the starter at room temperature for 30 minutes.

FOR THE DOUGH, combine the water, honey, and yeast in the bowl of a stand mixer. Stir to dissolve the yeast fully. Add the shortening, flour, salt, starter, and onion. Mix on low speed until the dough is fully developed. Remove the dough from the mixing bowl.

Divide the dough into 2 pieces weighing about 22 ounces each. Set aside any remaining dough and freeze for future use. Roll each piece of dough into a smooth ball. Place the dough on the counter or in a proofing basket and cover with a warm, damp cloth to rest at room temperature for 30 minutes. Preheat the oven to 400°F.

Form the dough into loaves, cover with a warm, damp cloth, and proof at room temperature for 30 minutes.

Score the loaves with a sharp knife, spray with water, and bake for 30 to 40 minutes, or until the crusts are a deep golden brown and the middle of the loaves is 190–200°F.

Remove the bread from the oven and place on a cooling rack for 30 minutes. If the bread was baked in loaf pans, remove the bread from the pans before cooling.

Potato Onion Rye Bread

MAKES 2 LOAVES

STARTER

1	cup (8.375 ounces) warm water (95–105°F.)
2	teaspoons (.25 ounce) fresh yeast
1	cup (4.875 ounces) dark rye flour

DOUGH

¾	cup (5.75 ounces) warm water (95–105°F.)
3	tablespoons (2 ounces) honey
4	teaspoons (.5 ounce) fresh yeast
¼	cup + 1 teaspoon (2 ounces) vegetable shortening
4¾	cups (23 ounces) all-purpose flour
1	tablespoon (.5 ounce) salt
	Starter
½	cup (1.75 ounces) dehydrated onion
1½	cups (6.826 ounces) raw diced potato

TO CREATE THE STARTER, combine the water and yeast in a medium mixing bowl. Stir to dissolve the yeast fully. Add the flour to the bowl and stir until the ingredients are fully incorporated. Cover with a cloth and ferment the starter at room temperature for 30 minutes.

FOR THE DOUGH, combine the water, honey, and yeast in the bowl of a stand mixer. Stir to dissolve the yeast fully. Add the shortening, flour, salt, starter, onion, and potato. Mix on low speed until the dough is fully developed. Remove the dough from the mixing bowl.

Divide the dough into 2 pieces weighing about 22 ounces each. Set aside any remaining dough and freeze for future use. Roll each piece of dough into a smooth ball. Place the dough on the counter or in a proofing basket and cover with a warm, damp cloth to rest at room temperature for 30 minutes. Preheat the oven to 400°F.

Form the dough into loaves, cover with a warm, damp cloth, and proof at room temperature for 30 minutes.

Score the loaves with a sharp knife, spray with water, and bake for 30 to 40 minutes, or until the crusts are a deep golden brown and the middle of the loaves is 190–200°F.

Remove the bread from the oven and place on a cooling rack for 30 minutes. If the bread was baked in loaf pans, remove the bread from the pans before cooling.

Rye Bread with Prosciutto

MAKES 2 LOAVES

STARTER

1	cup (8.375 ounces) warm water (95–105°F.)
2	teaspoons (.25 ounce) fresh yeast
1	cup (4.875 ounces) dark rye flour

DOUGH

1¼	cups (10 ounces) warm water (95–105°F.)
3	tablespoons (2 ounces) honey
4	teaspoons (.5 ounce) fresh yeast
¼	cup + 1 teaspoon (2 ounces) vegetable shortening
4¾	cups (23 ounces) all-purpose flour
1	tablespoon (.5 ounce) salt
	Starter
2	cups (9 ounces) ¼-inch-cubed prosciutto
1	tablespoon (.25 ounce) crushed black peppercorns

TO CREATE THE STARTER, combine the water and yeast in a medium mixing bowl. Stir to dissolve the yeast fully. Add the flour to the bowl and stir until the ingredients are fully incorporated. Cover with a cloth and ferment the starter at room temperature for 30 minutes.

FOR THE DOUGH, combine the water, honey, and yeast in the bowl of a stand mixer. Stir to dissolve the yeast fully. Add the shortening, flour, salt, starter, prosciutto, and peppercorns. Mix on low speed until the dough is fully developed. Remove the dough from the mixing bowl.

Divide the dough into 2 pieces weighing about 22 ounces each. Set aside any remaining dough and freeze for future use. Roll each piece of dough into a smooth ball. Place the dough on the counter or in a proofing basket and cover with a warm, damp cloth to rest at room temperature for 30 minutes. Preheat the oven to 400°F.

Form the dough into loaves, cover with a warm, damp cloth, and proof at room temperature for 30 minutes.

Score the loaves with a sharp knife, spray with water, and bake for 30 to 40 minutes, or until the crusts are a deep golden brown and the middle of the loaves is 190–200°F.

Remove the bread from the oven and place on a cooling rack for 30 minutes. If the bread was baked in loaf pans, remove the bread from the pans before cooling.

Rye Currant Bread

MAKES 2 LOAVES

STARTER

1	cup (8.375 ounces) warm water (95–105°F.)
2	teaspoons (.25 ounce) fresh yeast
1	cup (4.875 ounces) dark rye flour

DOUGH

¾	cup (5.75 ounces) warm water (95–105°F.)
3	tablespoons (2 ounces) honey
4	teaspoons (.5 ounce) fresh yeast
¼	cup + 1 teaspoon (2 ounces) vegetable shortening
4¾	cups (23 ounces) all-purpose flour
1	tablespoon (.5 ounce) salt
	Starter
2	cups (10.25 ounces) currants

TO CREATE THE STARTER, combine the water and yeast in a medium mixing bowl. Stir to dissolve the yeast fully. Add the flour to the bowl and stir until the ingredients are fully incorporated. Cover with a cloth and ferment the starter at room temperature for 30 minutes.

FOR THE DOUGH, combine the water, honey, and yeast in the bowl of a stand mixer. Stir to dissolve the yeast fully. Add the shortening, flour, salt, starter, and currants. Mix on low speed until the dough is fully developed. Remove the dough from the mixing bowl.

Divide the dough into 2 pieces weighing about 22 ounces each. Set aside any remaining dough and freeze for future use. Roll each piece of dough into a smooth ball. Place the dough on the counter or in a proofing basket and cover with a warm, damp cloth to rest at room temperature for 30 minutes. Preheat the oven to 400°F.

Form the dough into loaves, cover with a warm, damp cloth, and proof at room temperature for 30 minutes.

Score the loaves with a sharp knife, spray with water, and bake for 30 to 40 minutes, or until the crusts are a deep golden brown and the middle of the loaves is 190–200°F.

Remove the bread from the oven and place on a cooling rack for 30 minutes. If the bread was baked in loaf pans, remove the bread from the pans before cooling.

Advanced Bread Formulas

Once you are familiar with the steps of baking and the basic bread for-mulas, try experimenting with different ingredients and techniques to create unique tastes and textures of your own. We have included a sour-dough starter formula and three additional formulas that demonstrate how using a different variety of starter can drastically change the final product. The sourdough starter can be developed into a multi-use, or perpetual, starter, extending the fermentation process and adding layers of flavor and complexity to the bread.

Sourdough Starter

Bakers often create flavorful starters from naturally occuring bacteria found on the peel of grapes, berries, bananas, and potatoes. Most traditional "sour starters" are created in this way. It is important to leave the grapes unwashed because soap and water will reduce the amount of viable bacteria needed to leaven the dough. This starter is created in two stages.

MAKES 75 OUNCES

STAGE 1

1	cup (8.375 ounces) warm water (95–105°F.)
½	teaspoon (.07 ounce) fresh yeast
1	cup (8 ounces) buttermilk
1½	cups (12.33 ounces) plain yogurt
2	cups (9.75 ounces) all-purpose flour
⅓	cup (2 ounces) semolina flour
1	cup (2.5 ounces) unwashed medium red grapes

STAGE 2

	All stage 1 starter
2	cups (9.75 ounces) all-purpose flour
1	cup (4.875 ounces) semolina flour
½	teaspoon (.07 ounce) fresh yeast
2	cups (16 ounces) warm water (95–105°F.)

STAGE 1: Combine the warm water and fresh yeast in a medium mixing bowl. Stir to dissolve the yeast fully. Add the buttermilk, plain yogurt, all-purpose flour, and semolina flour to the bowl and stir until the ingredients are fully incorporated. Wrap the unwashed red grapes securely in a clean cheesecloth or small kitchen cloth and submerge the cloth in the mixture. Ferment at room temperature for 12 hours.

STAGE 2: Carefully remove the cloth with the grapes from the mixture, using a spatula to scrape any remaining starter off of the cloth and back into the bowl. Squeeze the cloth containing the grapes over the bowl, capturing the juice in the bowl. Discard the cloth and the grapes, and stir the starter until the grape juice is fully incorporated. Add the all-purpose flour and semolina flour to the starter. In a separate bowl, add the yeast to the warm water, stirring until the yeast is fully dissolved, then add this mixture to the starter. Mix the starter until all ingredients are fully incorporated. Ferment at room temperature for 4 hours before using, or cover and place in the refrigerator for future use.

PERPETUAL STARTERS

Sourdough starters often are kept in the refrigerator and allowed to ferment over an extended period of time, creating more complex, multi-layered flavor in the bread. A portion of the starter is then used every few days and replenished along the way with additional water and flour. Starters that are refrigerated and fed with flour and water over an extended period of time are called perpetual starters. If refrigerated and fed regularly, perpetual starters can be used indefinitely to create loaves with a consistent taste and texture. The sour starter formula above can be developed into a perpetual starter. Refrigerate the starter after the second stage. After removing the necessary amount of the starter for baking, add 2 cups of all-purpose flour, 1 cup of semolina flour, and ½ teaspoon fresh yeast dissolved in 2 cups warm water to the starter, stirring the mixture until all ingredients are fully incorporated. Place the bowl back in the refrigerator for future use. Feed every 4 to 6 days or after each use, allowing the mixture to ferment no less than 12 hours before using.

Sourdough Bread

MAKES 2 LOAVES

¾	cup (6 ounces) warm water (95–105°F.)
¾	teaspoon (.1 ounce) fresh yeast
1½	cups (10.5 ounces) Sourdough Starter (page 72)
1½	cups (7.3 ounces) all-purpose flour
1¼	cups (6 ounces) whole-wheat flour
1	tablespoon (.5 ounce) salt

COMBINE the warm water and fresh yeast in the bowl of a stand mixer. Stir to dissolve the yeast fully. Add the Sourdough Starter, flours, and salt. (Note: If refrigerated, bring Sourdough Starter to room temperature before using.) Mix on low speed until the dough is fully developed. Remove the dough from the mixing bowl. Roll the dough into a smooth ball, and place in a medium mixing bowl lightly brushed with olive oil. Cover and refrigerate for 16 hours. Remove the bowl from the refrigerator and ferment at room temperature for 6 hours.

Divide the dough into 2 equal pieces and form into loaves. Place the loaves on the counter or in a proofing basket and cover with a warm, damp cloth. Proof the loaves at room temperature for 2 hours. Preheat the oven to 400°F. Continue proofing the loaves at room temperature for 1 hour.

Score the loaves with a sharp knife, spray with water, and bake for 30 to 40 minutes, or until the crusts are a deep golden brown and the middle of the loaves is 190–200°F.

Remove the bread from the oven and place on a cooling rack for 30 minutes. If the bread was baked in loaf pans, remove the bread from the pans before cooling.

NOTE: For a more intense sour flavor, extend the refrigeration time of the dough an additional 6 to 8 hours.

Sourdough Challah Bread

MAKES 2 LOAVES

1	cup (8.5 ounces) warm buttermilk
4	teaspoons (.5 ounce) fresh yeast
3	large eggs
2	tablespoons + ½ teaspoon (1 ounce) unsalted butter
1½	tablespoons (1 ounce) honey
½	cup (3.5 ounces) Sourdough Starter (page 72)
4½	cups (22 ounces) all-purpose flour
½	cup + 1 tablespoon (2.8 ounces) semolina flour
¼	teaspoon (.04 ounce) ground cardamom
1	tablespoon (.5 ounce) salt

COMBINE the buttermilk and fresh yeast in the bowl of a stand mixer. Stir to dissolve the yeast fully. Add the eggs, unsalted butter, honey, Sourdough Starter, all-purpose flour, semolina flour, cardamom, and salt. (Note: If refrigerated, bring Sourdough Starter to room temperature before using.) Mix on low speed until the dough is fully developed. Remove the dough from the mixing bowl. Roll the dough into a smooth ball, and place in a medium mixing bowl lightly brushed with olive oil. Cover the bowl with a warm, damp cloth and ferment at room temperature for 3 hours.

Divide the dough into 2 equal pieces and form into loaves. Place the loaves on the counter or in a proofing basket and cover with a warm, damp cloth. Proof the loaves at room temperature for 1 hour. Preheat the oven to 400°F. Continue proofing the loaves at room temperature for 1 hour.

Score the loaves with a sharp knife, spray with water, and bake for 30 to 40 minutes, or until the crusts are a deep golden brown and the middle of the loaves is 190–200°F.

Remove the bread from the oven and place on a cooling rack for 30 minutes. If the bread was baked in loaf pans, remove the bread from the pans before cooling.

Sourdough French Bread

MAKES 2 LOAVES

1	cup (8 ounces) warm water (95–105°F.)
4	teaspoons (.5 ounce) fresh yeast
½	cup (3.5 ounces) Sourdough Starter (page 72)
2¾	cups + 1 tablespoon (14 ounces) all-purpose flour
2¼	teaspoons (.4 ounce) salt

COMBINE the warm water and fresh yeast in the bowl of a stand mixer. Stir to dissolve the yeast fully. Add the Sourdough Starter, flour, and salt. (Note: If refrigerated, bring Sourdough Starter to room temperature before using.) Mix on low speed until the dough is fully developed. Remove the dough from the mixing bowl. Roll the dough into a smooth ball, and place in a medium mixing bowl lightly brushed with olive oil. Cover the bowl with a warm, damp cloth and ferment at room temperature for 3 hours.

Divide the dough into 2 equal pieces and form into loaves. Place the loaves on the counter or in a proofing basket and cover with a warm, damp cloth. Proof the loaves at room temperature for 3 minutes . Preheat the oven to 400°F. Continue proofing the loaves at room temperature for 1 hour.

Score the loaves with a sharp knife, spray with water, and bake for 30 to 40 minutes, or until the crusts are a deep golden brown and the middle of the loaves is 190–200°F.

Remove the bread from the oven and place on a cooling rack for 30 minutes. If the bread was baked in loaf pans, remove the bread from the pans before cooling.

[PART TWO]

The Essential Ingredient: Bread-Based Recipes for Every Occasion

Too often, great bread is relegated to the sidelines during a meal. However, with a little bit of experimentation, bread can take center stage on the table for any meal of the day—from casseroles to crostini, fritters to fried chicken. We have developed more than 120 original recipes spanning appetizers; breakfast and brunch; sandwiches; soups, salads, and sides; and even desserts to tempt the taste buds and showcase the surprising flavors and textures that bread can add to nearly any dish.

Appetizers

Whether served for a starter during lunch or dinner or assembled as a light snack between meals, appetizers have a strong connection to bread. Bread is the canvas for crostini and bruschetta. Bread cubes linger in simmering fondue and sauté in garlic, mussels, and wine. Toast points carry littleneck clams and spicy hummus. Bread crumbs lend body to crab cakes and tartlets, and breadstick bouquets adorn the dinner table. As artisan loaves move from bread basket to finger food, people are finding a variety of new ways to enjoy one of the world's oldest staples.

Steamed Littleneck Clams
with Grilled Sourdough

These small, hard-shell clams do not need to be cooked very long—just enough to open the shells and infuse the beer flavor. When buying clams, make sure the shells are closed tightly. If a shell isn't closed, tap or squeeze the shell. If it does not close, the clam is dead and should be discarded.

SERVES 6

40	littleneck clams
¼	cup olive oil
1	medium yellow onion, thinly sliced
2	teaspoons minced garlic
1	tablespoon fresh thyme, or 2 teaspoons dried
2	Roma tomatoes, cut into ¼-inch dice
	Salt and freshly ground black pepper, to taste
¼	cup dry white wine
16	ounces Sweetwater 420 ale or any local microbrewed ale
1	10-inch boule Sourdough Bread (page 74), sliced ½ inch thick

PREHEAT oven or grill to 400°F. Clean the clams by running them under cold water to remove any sand or silt. Discard any dead ones.

In a large sauté pan, heat the oil over high heat until it shimmers. Sauté the onion until golden brown, 4 to 5 minutes. Add garlic, thyme, and tomatoes. Season with salt and pepper.

When the garlic starts to brown, deglaze the pan with the white wine. Add the clams and ale. Cover the pan with a lid. Continue cooking for 5 minutes and then remove from the heat. After the clams are cooked, discard any that are not fully open.

Brush both sides of the bread slices with olive oil. Toast on baking sheets in the oven or grill, until golden brown, about 5 minutes per side.

Using a slotted spoon, plate the clams and then top with some of the cooking liquid. Finish with a slice of bread on top.

Asiago Cheese Bread Chips
and Pico de Gallo

SERVES 10–12

PICO DE GALLO

6	fresh tomatoes, diced
1	fresh jalapeño pepper, minced
2	tablespoons fresh cilantro, chopped
1	small onion, diced
2	tablespoons garlic, minced
½	teaspoon ground cumin
2	tablespoons sugar
1	15-ounce can whole, peeled tomatoes, drained and coarsely chopped
¼	cup lime juice

BREAD CHIPS

2	loaves Asiago cheese bread, such as Panera Bread Asiago Cheese, sliced ½ inch thick
4	tablespoons (½ stick) butter, melted
4	garlic cloves, minced
	Salt, to taste

FOR THE PICO DE GALLO, in a large, non-reactive bowl, combine the fresh tomatoes, jalapeño, cilantro, onion, garlic, cumin, and sugar. Add the canned tomatoes and lime juice and combine. Cover and refrigerate several hours or overnight.

TO PREPARE THE BREAD CHIPS, preheat oven to 350°F. Lay the slices on a baking sheet. Brush lightly with melted butter and sprinkle bread with garlic and salt. Bake for 20 minutes. Cool chips on the baking sheet. Serve with pico de gallo. Store leftovers in an airtight container or resealable bag.

Bagel Fondue

First created in Switzerland, fondue got its name from the French word fondre, *meaning "to melt." Fondue became the cornerstone of dinner parties in this country in the 1960s, where guests would gather around a pot to cook meat cubes in hot oil, dip slices of bread into melted cheese, or spear pieces of fruit or cake for chocolate fondues. This new American version of a cheese fondue uses beer in place of the more traditional white wine. You also can experiment with different cheeses in this dish, such as Emmenthaler and Gruyère.*

SERVES 4

6	bagels
6	ounces beer, ale, or lager
1	small garlic clove
6	ounces Swiss cheese, grated
6	ounces sharp Cheddar cheese, grated
1	tablespoon all-purpose flour
	Freshly ground black pepper, to taste
	Paprika and chopped fresh parsley, for garnish

CUT the bagels into ½-inch cubes. Pour the beer into a heavy-bottomed saucepan set over low heat. Put the garlic through a garlic press and add to the beer. Place both grated cheeses into a bowl, sprinkle the flour over them, and toss until the cheese is coated. Slowly whisk the cheese into the beer mixture, whisking constantly until thick and smooth. Do not boil. Season with pepper and pour the mixture into a fondue pot. Sprinkle with paprika and parsley. Using fondue forks or toothpicks, spear the bagel cubes, dip them into the fondue, and enjoy!

Classic Bruschetta

From the Italian word bruscare, *meaning "to roast over coals," this appetizer is made by toasting bread and topping it with many different items, from tomatoes to fruit. Bruschetta originated as a means of checking the quality of the new season's olive oil.*

SERVES 4

½	Italian loaf or Panera Bread Asiago Cheese
3	whole garlic cloves
4	Roma tomatoes
½	cup fresh basil chiffonade, packed
2	tablespoons olive oil
	Salt and freshly ground black pepper, to taste

PREHEAT oven or grill to 400°F. Slice the bread on a 45-degree bias in ½-inch sections. Toast on baking sheets in the oven, or grill, until golden brown, about 5 minutes per side. Vigorously rub the garlic cloves onto the toasted bread.

Cut the tomatoes into ¼-inch cubes and toss with the basil and oil. Season with salt and pepper. Set aside for 30 minutes to 1 hour to allow the flavors to combine.

Evenly distribute the tomato mixture over toast slices and serve immediately. If you let the bread sit for too long with the tomato mixture on it, the bread will become very soggy.

INTERNATIONAL BREAD BITE: ITALY

The distinguishing feature of most Italian breads is the shape of the loaf rather than the actual dough. Most Italian-based loaves rely on the shaping, scoring, and method of baking to distinguish one bread from another. The distinctive flavor of these regional breads is aided by the addition of olive oil into the basic formula—this addition also adds extra nourishment, extending the longevity of the artisan loaves. Ciabatta, pagnotta, and focaccia are known as the national breads of Italy—all made with the same basic formula but with markedly different outcomes, tastes, and textures.

An often overlooked and frequently debated Italian bread original is the pizza. Many nations claim that theirs was the first pizza, but history best supports the Italian lineage. Around 1000 BC in northern Italy, the ancient Etruscans began to bake a flat bread beneath stones on a hearth. For centuries, this bread was known as a *picea*. In 1522, tomatoes arrived in Italy from Spain, but for the next hundred years the common misconception was that they were poisonous. As this fear subsided, mozzarella cheese was slowly growing in popularity. All of the ingredients were in place, but not until 1889 did they meet. For a royal party, Queen Margherita ordered a local chef to create a new dish. In an act of patriotism, the chef designed a pizza made of red tomatoes, white cheese, and green basil to match the colors of the Italian flag. The birth of the pizza was complete.

Chanterelle and Shallot Bruschetta

Chanterelles are trumpet-shaped wild mushrooms with a color that ranges from bright yellow to orange. The chanterelle has a delicate, nutty flavor and a somewhat chewy texture. Chanterelles tend to toughen when overcooked.

SERVES 4

½	medium baguette
2	tablespoons (¼ stick) salted butter
½	pound chanterelle mushrooms
2	shallots, thinly sliced
1	tablespoon fresh thyme or 1 teaspoon dried
	Salt and freshly ground black pepper, to taste
2	tablespoons dry white wine

PREHEAT oven or grill to 400°F. Slice bread on a 45-degree angle in ½-inch sections. Divide 1 tablespoon butter to spread evenly over both sides of the slices of bread. Toast on baking sheets in the oven, or grill, on both sides until golden brown, about 5 minutes per side.

To clean the chanterelles, hold the mushroom in your hand with the cap up. Use a paring knife to remove the outer skin on the stem if it is brown, cut out any bad spots, and remove any dirt or leaves. Do *not* rinse the mushrooms in water. Slice the cleaned mushrooms into ¼-inch slices.

In a medium, non-stick sauté pan, melt the remaining butter over high heat and sauté the shallots until translucent, 1 to 2 minutes. Add the mushrooms and thyme and season with salt and pepper. After the mushrooms have released most of their water (3 to 4 minutes), deglaze the pan with the wine and continue cooking until the liquid has evaporated. Evenly distribute over toast slices and serve immediately.

Chipotle Roasted Oyster Bruschetta

Chipotle peppers are jalapeño peppers that have been smoked and then dried. For this recipe, look for the chipotles packed in adobo sauce, which is made from ground chiles, garlic, oregano, and cumin. When shopping for oysters, it is best to find and use a trusted local fishmonger for your product. If you aren't experienced at shucking oysters, have the monger shuck them for you. Be sure to use them the same day you buy them and keep them on ice until preparation.

SERVES 4

½	medium baguette
¼	cup olive oil
1	chipotle pepper
8	oysters, freshly shucked
1	tablespoon adobo sauce
	Salt and freshly ground black pepper, to taste
	Fresh cilantro, chopped, for garnish

PREHEAT oven or grill to 400°F. Slice the bread on a hard 45-degree bias into ½-inch sections. Brush each side with olive oil and toast on baking sheets in the oven, or grill, until each side is golden brown, about 5 minutes per side.

Thinly slice the chipotle pepper and toss with the shucked oysters, adobo sauce, and remaining oil. Season with salt and black pepper. Transfer mixture to a shallow roasting pan and roast oysters for 5 to 7 minutes. The oysters should not be completely cooked when served. If over-cooked, they will become tough and chewy.

Evenly distribute the oysters and sauce over the toast slices, garnish with cilantro, and serve immediately.

Smoked Trout with Cherries and Marjoram

When buying fresh trout fillets, you should look for a fish that is white or pinkish white, free from any brown spots or areas that appear to be dry. As with all seafood, the fish should have only the fresh smell of seawater, not a pronounced or offensive "fishy" aroma. If you don't have a smoker, you can purchase a high-quality smoked trout from your local gourmet or specialty food store.

SERVES 4

½	medium baguette
¼	cup olive oil
½	pound fresh trout fillets
	Salt and freshly ground black pepper, to taste
⅔	cup fresh cherries, pitted and coarsely chopped
1	tablespoon fresh marjoram, finely chopped, or 1 teaspoon dried

PREHEAT oven or grill to 400°F. Slice the bread on a 45-degree bias into ½-inch sections. Brush both sides of the bread with olive oil, and toast on baking sheets in the oven, or grill, until both sides are golden brown, about 5 minutes per side.

Rinse the trout fillets in cold water and pat dry. Drizzle half the remaining oil over the fillets and season with salt and pepper. Place in smoker, flesh side up, and smoke for 7 to 10 minutes. When fully cooked, the meat should be flaky and break easily. Cool and remove skin.

In a medium bowl, combine the cherries, marjoram, and remaining olive oil. Season with salt and pepper. Lightly toss the trout with the cherry mixture, breaking up the fish into pieces but not crushing it. You want whole chunks of trout, not a paste.

Evenly distribute the trout mixture over the toast slices and serve warm.

Bruschetta with Goat Cheese, Garlic, and Tomatoes

SERVES 4

½   medium baguette
2   tablespoons olive oil
1   large garlic clove, minced
4   Roma tomatoes, seeded and chopped
1   teaspoon fresh lemon juice
     Salt and pepper, to taste
4   ounces soft, fresh goat cheese, such as Montrachet
2   tablespoons fresh basil or mint, chopped

PREHEAT the oven or grill to 400°F. Slice the bread on a 45-degree bias into ½-inch sections. Brush both sides of the bread with olive oil, and toast on baking sheets in the oven, or grill, until both sides are golden brown, about 5 minutes per side. Reduce oven to 350°F.

In a medium, non-reactive bowl, combine garlic, tomatoes, and lemon juice. Season with salt and pepper.

Spread goat cheese over toasts and arrange on baking sheet. Spoon tomato-garlic mixture onto toasts, dividing equally. Bake until heated through, about 8 minutes. Sprinkle with basil or mint. Serve immediately.

MAKE YOUR OWN BREAD CRUMBS

Bread crumbs, or *chapelure,* as they're called in French, are available at the store, but there is really no need to buy them when you can quickly, easily, and cheaply make them yourself. As most people who cook know, bread can and will go stale, but there is no need to discard it. Rather, give it a second life by making your own bread crumbs.

WHEN USED AS A GARNISH OR IN A DISH:

Pulse bread in a food processor until broken into small pieces, about 30 seconds to 1 minute. Add a small amount of olive oil and any dried spices of your liking along with salt and pepper and transfer the mixture to a large baking sheet. Place sheet in a preheated 350°F. oven for 10 minutes. If needed, rotate the sheet 180° and bake an additional 3 to 5 minutes or until golden brown.

WHEN USED AS A COATING:

For this bread crumb version we are trying to achieve a smaller and drier crumb, so the following technique should be used to achieve this result. Preheat oven to 500°F. Place bread slices on a sheet pan and toast for 3 to 5 minutes. Shut off oven and leave bread in the oven for at least 4 hours and as long as overnight. This will achieve a thorough drying of the bread. Remove bread from sheet pan and place in a food processor with salt, pepper, and any dried herb. Pulse for 30 seconds to 1 minute.

Crab Cakes with Horseradish and Avocado Vinaigrette

The bread crumbs from a quality sourdough bread add a mild, tangy flavor to the crab cakes. The dressing also works well with chicory or endive salads. If you can't find fresh horseradish, use bottled, but add in small amounts and taste frequently because the bottled variety is much spicier.

SERVES 4

1	pound crab meat, jumbo lump
½	cup mayonnaise
½	teaspoon chili powder
¼	teaspoon ground cayenne pepper
1	teaspoon Old Bay seasoning
2	teaspoons Dijon mustard
1	large egg, lightly beaten
½	cup sourdough bread crumbs, coarsely ground
½	cup vegetable oil
	Salt and freshly ground black pepper, to taste
	Horseradish and Avocado Vinaigrette (recipe follows)

PREHEAT oven to 375°F. Drain the crabmeat of packing liquid. Pick through the meat and discard any remaining shell pieces.

Combine mayonnaise, chili powder, cayenne pepper, Old Bay seasoning, and mustard in a large mixing bowl. Mix well and adjust seasonings. Fold crabmeat and egg into the mixture; be sure not to break up the meat too much. Fold in bread crumbs. Form mixture into 8 medium-size patties approximately 3 inches in diameter.

Heat oil in a large ovenproof skillet until it shimmers. Sear the crab cakes until golden brown and a light crust has formed, about 2 to 3 minutes per side. Finish in the oven for 7 to 10 minutes to heat through.

Season to taste with salt and pepper and serve warm with the vinaigrette.

Horseradish and Avocado Vinaigrette

MAKES 2 CUPS

½   cup champagne vinegar
2   tablespoons horseradish, freshly grated
    Juice of 1 lime
1   ripe avocado, peeled and halved
    Salt and freshly ground black pepper, to taste
1   cup olive oil
2   tablespoons fresh chives, finely chopped

PLACE vinegar, horseradish, lime juice, and half the avocado in a blender and pulse until smooth. Season with salt and pepper. Slowly pour oil into blender to emulsify the dressing. Be careful not to overblend or the dressing will become too thick.

Dice the remaining avocado half. Mix the dressing with the chives and avocado and drizzle over the crab cakes to taste.

Crostini

Crostini are considered members of the bruschetta family. While the larger bruschetta are slices of country bread that are grilled or toasted, crostini literally means "little crusts." Crostini are usually small enough to serve as hors d'oeuvres—the larger bruschetta can serve as an appetizer or even a light meal.

SERVES 4

1   loaf Sourdough French Bread (page 77), Rye Bread (page 64), or Three-Cheese Bread (page 54), sliced 1 inch thick
Extra-virgin olive oil

1   large garlic clove, halved lengthwise

1   heaping tablespoon Artichoke Crostini Topping, Mushroom Crostini Topping, or Eggplant and Roasted Red Pepper Crostini Topping (recipes follow)

PLACE a large non-stick skillet over medium heat. Brush both sides of the bread slices with olive oil and place a few at a time in the hot skillet. Toast for 2 minutes, turning often, until browned and firm. Rub the cut side of the garlic on the bread toasts to infuse a subtle flavor. Top each piece of toast with the topping and serve immediately.

Mushroom Crostini Topping

The recipe also can be prepared with shiitake, crimini, porcini, portobello, or any mushrooms that you and your family may enjoy. The greater the variety of mushrooms, the greater the depth of taste for the dish.

SERVES 4

2	tablespoons extra-virgin olive oil
1	shallot, thinly sliced
2	garlic cloves, thinly sliced
1	teaspoon fresh rosemary, chopped
8	ounces button mushrooms, sliced
	Kosher salt and freshly ground black pepper, to taste

PLACE a skillet over medium heat and coat with the olive oil. Add the shallot, garlic, and rosemary. Sauté for 1 minute to soften. Add the mushrooms and season with salt and pepper. Continue to cook, stirring, until the mushrooms are soft and brown, about 10 minutes.

Artichoke Crostini Topping

SERVES 4

1	15-ounce can artichoke hearts packed in water, drained and rinsed
1	cup fresh flat-leaf parsley, coarsely chopped
	Zest of 1 lemon, finely grated
2	garlic cloves, coarsely chopped
¼	cup extra-virgin olive oil
¼	cup Parmesan cheese, shredded (optional)

PLACE all of the ingredients in a food processor and pulse until combined.

Eggplant and Roasted Red Pepper Crostini Topping

SERVES 4

1	medium eggplant, unpeeled
1	red bell pepper
3	garlic cloves, unpeeled
½	cup extra-virgin olive oil
1	tablespoon balsamic vinegar
2	tablespoons fresh oregano, chopped
	Kosher salt and freshly ground black pepper, to taste

PREHEAT the oven to 450°F. Rub the eggplant, bell pepper, and garlic with one half of the olive oil and place them on a baking sheet lined with aluminum foil on the middle oven rack. Roast the vegetables, turning occasionally, for about 40 minutes. The pepper should be charred and the eggplant completely soft.

Allow the vegetables to cool, and then peel the skin off the pepper, discarding the stem and seeds. Put the roasted pepper in the bowl of a food processor. Coarsely chop the eggplant, discarding the stem, and add it to the processor. Squeeze the garlic out of their skins into the processor. Add the vinegar, oregano, and the remaining ¼ cup oil; season with salt and pepper. Pulse until combined but still somewhat chunky.

French Bread Margherita Pizza

This recipe is great for parties or quick weeknight suppers. Look for fresh buffalo mozzarella cheese, which adds just the right tang and creaminess.

SERVES 6

1	loaf French bread, cut in half lengthwise, then into thirds
1½	cups canned tomato sauce or canned whole, peeled tomatoes, chopped
½	cup fresh basil chiffonade, lightly packed
3	large Roma tomatoes, sliced
16	ounces mozzarella cheese, sliced
	Salt and freshly ground black pepper, to taste

PREHEAT oven to 475°F. Lightly toast the bread for 5 minutes. Spoon the tomato sauce over the bread. Top with the basil, then tomato slices, then the cheese. Bake for 12 to 15 minutes. Broil for 1 to 2 minutes to brown the tops.

Sopresatta and Fontina Pizza

Sopresatta is a traditional Italian meat similar to salami that pairs perfectly with Fontina cheese. Fontina is a good melting cheese with a rather pronounced flavor and aroma. Both sopresatta and Fontina can be found at a gourmet food shop or at your local Italian grocer.

SERVES 6

1	loaf French bread, cut in half lengthwise, then into thirds
1½	cups tomato sauce
½	pound sopresatta, sliced
1½	cups Fontina cheese, grated

PREHEAT oven to 475°F. Lightly toast bread for 5 minutes. Spoon the tomato sauce on the bread. Top with the sopresatta, then the cheese. Bake for 12 to 15 minutes and then broil for 1 to 2 minutes to brown tops.

Herbed Cheese Bread Sticks

This versatile recipe can be served with anything from filet mignon to spaghetti and meatballs.

SERVES 6

1	10-inch boule Sourdough Bread (page 74)
½	teaspoon garlic, minced
1	tablespoon fresh oregano, basil, or dill, finely chopped
8	tablespoons (1 stick) unsalted butter, melted
½	cup Parmesan or Romano cheese, freshly grated

PREHEAT oven to 350°F. Starting at the top, slice down through the loaf, stopping about 1 inch from the bottom (don't cut all the way through!). Continue to cut slices approximately 1 inch apart until you have sliced the entire loaf. Rotate the bread a quarter turn and slice in the same manner, creating a checkerboard across the original cuts. Place the bread on a piece of foil. Mix the garlic and herbs into the melted butter. Pour the butter mixture over the loaf and down between the bread sticks. Top with cheese and close foil securely over loaf. Place in the oven or on top of a grill for 10 to 15 minutes, until browned.

ſ

Goat Cheese Tartlets
with Caramelized Onion and Figs

These tartlets are essentially miniature savory cheesecakes. You can make these up to 1 week in advance. Just freeze the baked tartlets in an airtight container and allow to thaw in the refrigerator before serving.

SERVES 10–12

CARAMELIZED ONIONS

1	tablespoon extra-virgin olive oil
1	large sweet yellow onion, halved and thinly sliced
1	tablespoon fresh thyme, chopped
	Salt and freshly ground black pepper, to taste

ALMOND CRUST

2	cups whole-wheat bread crumbs
½	cup Parmigiano-Reggiano cheese, grated
4	tablespoons (½ stick) unsalted butter, melted
¼	cup almonds, blanched and finely chopped
	Salt and freshly ground black pepper, to taste

CHEESECAKE FILLING

12	ounces fresh goat cheese, softened
12	ounces cream cheese, softened
	Zest of 1 lemon, grated
4	large eggs
1	cup heavy cream
12	fresh figs, quartered

PREHEAT the oven to 450°F. To caramelize the onion, heat the oil in a large sauté pan over medium heat. Add the onion and thyme. Season with salt and pepper. Stir until the onion is coated. Continue cooking, stirring only occasionally, until the onion is a deep amber color. Remove from the pan, and set aside to cool.

TO MAKE THE CRUST, combine bread crumbs, cheese, butter, and almonds in a medium bowl or the bowl of a food processor. Season with salt and pepper.

FOR THE FILLING, in a separate bowl or the bowl of a stand mixer, blend the cheeses until smooth. Add the zest and the eggs, one at a time, blending until smooth again. Then add the heavy cream, blending until smooth.

Grease minimuffin cups and place in a 24-cup minimuffin pan. Press 2 tablespoons of the crumb mixture evenly into each cup, and then fill two-thirds of the way up with the filling. Distribute the caramelized onion evenly atop the filling. Transfer the pan to the oven and immediately reduce the heat to 350°F. Bake until the filling has set, 15 to 20 minutes. Serve slightly warm or at room temperature with figs.

Green Curry Shrimp Toast

The Kaffir lime, lemongrass, and chile flavors add a Thai twist to this classic Cantonese dim sum. You could, of course, substitute a good-quality, prepared green curry paste like Maesri if you can't find these ingredients fresh. To devein the lime leaves, use a sharp paring knife to carefully cut out the center stalk and discard.

SERVES 4–6 (MAKES 24 TOAST POINTS)

4	Kaffir lime leaves, deveined
1	stalk lemongrass, peeled and thinly sliced into rings (base half only—the lower half of the stalk that is lighter yellow/green in color)
1	bird or serrano chile, seeded and sliced
¼	cup fresh cilantro leaves, loosely packed
1	1-inch knob fresh ginger, peeled and sliced
1	large garlic clove, sliced
½	pound large raw shrimp, peeled and deveined (tails removed)
2	tablespoons fresh lime juice
1	large egg white
1	tablespoon cornstarch
1	teaspoon salt
6	slices Country White Bread (page 48) or Sourdough Bread (page 74), crusts removed and cut diagonally to make 4 triangles per slice
	Canola or peanut oil for frying (enough to achieve a 2 to 3 inch depth in wok)

COMBINE lime leaves, lemongrass, half of the chile, the cilantro, ginger, garlic, shrimp, lime juice, egg white, cornstarch, and salt in the bowl of a medium food processor and pulse several times to make a moderately chunky paste that is easy to spread. (If you do not own a food processor, you should finely chop the lime leaves, lemongrass, chile, cilantro, ginger, garlic, and shrimp before mixing in the lime juice, egg white, cornstarch, and salt.) Spread the paste evenly across each triangle of bread.

Heat the oil to 350°F in a wok or deep skillet. Fry the triangles for 1 to 2 minutes on each side and then remove to drain on paper towels. Garnish with remaining slices of chile peppers, if you like. Serve warm.

Red Lentil Hummus with Kalamata Olive Bread

This Middle Eastern pairing of lentils and kalamata olives is not only visually spectacular, but also a traditionally inspired native dish. Inexpensive and quick to prepare, you will not be disappointed with the depth and complexity of the flavors.

SERVES 6–8

3	cups cooked red lentils
1	red bell pepper, roasted, peeled, and seeded
1	garlic clove, minced
¼	cup tahini
¼	cup fresh lemon or lime juice
2	teaspoons ground cumin
1	teaspoon ground cayenne pepper
¼	cup extra-virgin olive oil
	Salt and freshly ground black pepper, to taste
1	loaf Kalamata Olive Bread (page 52), sliced ½ inch thick and toasted
	Fresh parsley, chopped, for garnish

COMBINE lentils, bell pepper, garlic, tahini, lemon juice, cumin, and cayenne pepper in the bowl of a food processor. Begin pureeing, and add the oil in a slow, steady stream until all is thoroughly incorporated. Season with salt and pepper and spread onto toasted olive bread. Drizzle with more oil and garnish with parsley.

Oysters Rockefeller with Pancetta Herb Vinaigrette

If you are not up to shucking your own oysters, ask your local fishmonger to shuck them for you. Be certain to tell them that you would like the liquid reserved for use in this recipe. If you plan to attempt the shucking yourself, be aware that keeping the liquid from spilling while opening the oyster will take some skill, but with a little practice you will gain some confidence. Before incorporating the reserved liquid into the recipe, strain it through a coffee filter to remove any impurities.

SERVES 6–8

VINAIGRETTE

3	tablespoons extra-virgin olive oil
6	slices pancetta, sliced ¼ inch thick
1	tablespoon lemon juice
1	tablespoon Dijon mustard
1	teaspoon Tabasco sauce
1	tablespoon fresh tarragon, finely chopped
1	tablespoon fresh parsley, finely chopped
1	tablespoon fresh chives, finely chopped

OYSTERS

1	small bunch spinach, washed and chopped
1	cup white or sourdough bread crumbs
16	oysters (preferably Bluepoint or Malbec), shucked, liquid and bottom of shells reserved
	Salt and freshly ground black pepper to taste
	Rock salt
2	tablespoons crème fraîche or sour cream

PREHEAT the broiler. To make the vinaigrette, heat the oil in a medium skillet and pan-fry the pancetta, about 2 minutes per side. Remove to paper towels to drain, reserving the pan drippings. Whisk together the lemon juice, mustard, Tabasco sauce, and herbs. Finely dice the pancetta and add to the mixture. Continue whisking while adding the oil from the pan in a slow, steady stream until thoroughly incorporated.

TO PREPARE THE OYSTERS, toss the spinach, bread crumbs, reserved oyster liquid, and vinaigrette in a medium bowl. Season well with salt and black pepper. Place the oyster bottom halves in a medium broiling pan. Discard the top shells. Top each oyster with a generous amount of the spinach mixture. Broil for 3 to 5 minutes, or until a crust begins to form. Serve the oysters warm on a plate of rock salt and top each oyster with a dollop of crème fraîche or sour cream.

Quick Citrus-Cured Salmon on Dill Crostini

This abbreviated technique of making gravlax comes by way of French American master chef Jacques Pépin. Citrus salt adds a bit of fruitiness without "cooking" the salmon flesh. This and all salmon recipes are recommended to be made with wild salmon, of which steelhead trout is typically a smaller variety.

SERVES 10–12

CURE MIXTURE

1 tablespoon kosher salt

1 teaspoon sugar

½ teaspoon freshly ground black pepper

Zest of 1 lime

Zest of 1 lemon

Zest of 1 orange

Zest of 1 grapefruit

1 2-pound salmon fillet, skin removed, or 2 steelhead trout fillets, skin removed

CROSTINI

1 baguette, sliced ½ inch thick

1 bunch fresh dill, finely chopped

Extra-virgin olive oil

2 tablespoons capers

1 tablespoon red onion, minced

8 dill leaves

¼ cup extra-virgin olive oil

TO PREPARE THE CURE, in a small bowl combine the salt, sugar, pepper, and zests. Sprinkle about 1 teaspoon evenly onto a large, flat dinner plate.

Using a salmon knife or other long, flexible, sharp knife, slice the salmon crosswise as thinly as possible while retaining the muscle structure. Lay these slices directly onto the seasoned plate without overlapping; you may need more than one plate. When finished slicing, season the tops of the slices with the remaining cure, then cover tightly with plastic wrap, pressing the film directly onto the salmon. Cure in the refrigerator for at least 1 hour and up to 24 hours. The longer the fish cures, the more robust the flavor will be. Anything longer than 24 hours will toughen the flesh and diminish the texture and taste.

TO MAKE THE CROSTINI, preheat oven to 400°F. In a large bowl, toss the bread slices with the dill and drizzle with oil to distribute evenly. Lay them flat on a baking sheet; toast in the oven for 5 to 7 minutes, or until crisp. Cool.

To serve, lay 1 or 2 salmon slices on each crostini and garnish with the capers, onion, dill, and oil.

Quick Pastrami-Cured Salmon with Sauerkraut on Rye Toast with Creole Remoulade

The flavors of a classic Reuben sandwich . . . turned inside out. This and all salmon recipes are recommended to be made with wild salmon, of which steelhead trout is typically a smaller variety.

SERVES 10–12

CURE MIXTURE

1 tablespoon kosher salt

1 teaspoon sugar

1 tablespoon freshly ground black pepper

1 tablespoon paprika

1 tablespoon ground coriander seed

1 teaspoon ground cayenne pepper

1 tablespoon molasses

1 2-pound salmon fillet, skin removed, or 2 steelhead trout fillets, skin removed

CREOLE REMOULADE

¾ cup mayonnaise

1 tablespoon Tabasco sauce

1 tablespoon Dijon mustard

1 tablespoon capers, minced

1 tablespoon shallot, minced

1 tablespoon cornichon or dill pickle, minced

1 tablespoon fresh tarragon, parsley, or chives, finely chopped (optional)

RYE TOAST POINTS

6 slices Rye Bread (page 64), crusts removed and cut diagonally to make 4 triangles per slice
Extra-virgin olive oil

¼ cup deli fresh sauerkraut

2 tablespoons fresh chives, chopped

TO PREPARE THE CURE, in a small bowl, combine the salt, sugar, spices, and molasses. Sprinkle about 1 teaspoon evenly onto a large, flat dinner plate.

Using a salmon knife or other long, flexible, sharp knife, slice the salmon crosswise as thinly as possible while retaining the muscle structure. Lay slices directly onto the seasoned plate without overlapping; you may need more than one plate. When finished slicing, season the tops of the slices with the remaining cure, then cover tightly with plastic wrap, pressing the film directly onto the salmon. Cure in the refrigerator for at least 1 hour and up to 24 hours. The longer the fish cures, the more robust the flavor will be. Anything longer than 24 hours will diminish the texture and flavor of the dish.

TO MAKE THE CREOLE REMOULADE, combine all of the ingredients in a small bowl. Mix well and refrigerate.

TO MAKE THE TOAST POINTS, preheat oven or grill to 400°F. In a large bowl, toss the rye triangles with oil to lightly coat. Toast the bread on baking sheets in the oven, or grill, until golden brown, about 5 minutes per side. Cool.

To serve, spread ½ teaspoon of the remoulade on each toast point, top with a slice or two of the salmon, and garnish with sauerkraut and chives. Reserve the remaining remoulade for another use, storing it in an airtight container in the refrigerator.

Spicy Chickpea Fritters with Eggplant "Caviar"

The eggplant prepared in this recipe has the same sheen and sodium-driven punch of a fish egg caviar while retaining Middle Eastern flavors similar to that of baba ganoush. These fritters are equally tasty eaten like falafel in a sandwich with lettuce, tomato, and yogurt sauce. Ras el hanout, *meaning "head of the shop," is usually characterized by the presence of cumin, coriander, chile, turmeric, cardamom, clove, and ginger. This blend can be found at specialty grocers and gourmet shops.*

SERVES 4–6

EGGPLANT "CAVIAR"

1	large eggplant, unpeeled
4	whole garlic cloves, unpeeled
1	bird or serrano chile
1	sprig fresh rosemary
¼	cup extra-virgin olive oil
	Salt and freshly ground black pepper, to taste
	Zest and juice of 1 lemon
1	tablespoon mint, finely chopped

FRITTERS

1	pound chickpeas, cooked, or 1 16-ounce can
1	garlic clove, minced
1	tablespoon *ras el hanout* or other Moroccan-style spice blend
1	bird or serrano chile, seeded and minced
2	tablespoons tahini
1	large egg, beaten
¼	cup fresh cilantro or parsley, finely chopped
½	cup bread crumbs, preferably focaccia
	Salt and freshly ground black pepper to taste
	Canola or peanut oil for shallow frying (enough to fill skillet to a depth of 1 inch)

TO MAKE THE "CAVIAR," preheat oven to 400°F. Prick the eggplant several times with a fork, and then rub the eggplant, garlic, chile, and rosemary with 2 tablespoons oil and a generous amount of salt and pepper. Roast these together in a small pan for 45 minutes, or until the eggplant is soft throughout. Set aside to cool slightly for about 15 minutes. While still warm, carefully scrape the pulp from the eggplant into the bowl of a food processor. Squeeze the garlic from their skins and add to the bowl along with the rosemary, chile, lemon zest, juice, remaining oil, and mint. Pulse several times until the eggplant is shiny and approximately the size of lentils. Season with salt and pepper, and set aside while preparing the fritters.

TO MAKE THE FRITTERS, preheat the oil in a wok or deep skillet pan to 350°F. Combine the chickpeas, garlic, *ras el hanout,* chile, tahini, egg, cilantro, and half of the bread crumbs in the bowl of a food processor. Pulse until a smooth dough is formed. With oiled hands, pat the dough into 2-inch-diameter cakes. Roll the patted cakes in the remaining bread crumbs and fry about 2 minutes per side, or until golden brown. Transfer to paper towels to drain. Serve warm or at room temperature with the eggplant spooned on top.

Breakfast/Brunch

Bread is no stranger to the breakfast table. Served with butter and jelly or as bagels, cinnamon rolls, muffins, and pastries, bread is the morning staple of cultures around the world. The artisan movement has awakened opportunities for bread to be used in other breakfast and brunch favorites. No longer restricted to French toast and eggs Benedict, artisan loaves are moving into quiches, stratas, and casseroles, lending a new complexity to these favorite dishes.

Asiago Bagel Breakfast Bake

This dish should be assembled the night before you plan to bake it.

SERVES 8–10

8	large eggs
¼	teaspoon salt
2	cups whole milk
1	tablespoon fresh tarragon, chopped, or ½ teaspoon dried
¼	teaspoon paprika
	Freshly ground black pepper, to taste
6	ounces Monterey Jack or medium Cheddar cheese, grated
6	ounces Asiago cheese, grated
4	Asiago cheese bagels or plain bagels

IN A LARGE MIXING BOWL, beat together the eggs, salt, milk, tarragon, and paprika. Season with pepper. Mix the grated cheeses together in a bowl. Cut the bagels into bite-size pieces. Grease a 2-quart soufflé or casserole dish. Starting with the bagel pieces, alternately layer bagel pieces and grated cheese into the dish. Pour the egg mixture evenly over everything, cover the dish, and refrigerate overnight. Preheat oven to 350°F. Bake, uncovered, for 1 hour, until the top is golden brown.

Broiled Fruit Toast with Vanilla Yogurt

Almost any firm fruit will work in this recipe. Make sure to buy whatever is in season, the freshest and ripest. Whipped cream or soy yogurt can replace the yogurt. You can also use a fruit-flavored yogurt.

SERVES 6

2	tablespoons (¼ stick) unsalted butter
6	slices Honey Wheat Bread (page 56)
3	tablespoons honey
1	teaspoon vanilla extract
1	cup plain yogurt, plus extra for garnish
1	tablespoon fresh mint chiffonade
	Zest and juice of 1 Valencia orange
¼	cup cranberry juice
1	tablespoon sugar
1	teaspoon salt
¼	medium cantaloupe, cut into ½-inch cubes
¼	medium honeydew melon, cut into ½-inch cubes
1	peach, cored, cut into ½-inch cubes
1	pear, cored, cut into ½-inch cubes
6	strawberries, hulled and halved lengthwise
2	nectarines, cored, cut into ½-inch cubes

PREHEAT oven to 400°F. Spread butter on each slice of bread and toast on baking sheets in the oven until golden brown, about 5 minutes per side. Cut the slices of bread in half to form triangles.

In a small bowl, combine 1 tablespoon honey, the vanilla extract, yogurt, and mint. Set aside.

In a medium bowl, whisk together orange zest, orange juice, cranberry juice, remaining honey, sugar, and salt. Toss fruit in juice mixture. Place fruit evenly in one layer in a large baking dish and bake for 5 minutes. Spread warm mixture over toasts and broil for 3 to 5 minutes until the sugars begin to caramelize. Finish with a dollop of yogurt and serve.

Herbed Focaccia Strata

SERVES 6

6	tablespoons (¾ stick) unsalted butter
½	cup chopped onion
4	ounces button mushrooms, thinly sliced
1	16-ounce package frozen chopped spinach, thawed, or 2 pounds fresh spinach, stems removed, blanched and chopped
2	tablespoons fresh basil, chopped
	Salt and freshly ground black pepper, to taste
5	large eggs
4	cups half-and-half or whole milk
2	pans basil Focaccia Bread (page 53) or Panera Bread Basil Pesto Focaccia, cut in half
1	cup mozzarella, shredded
½	cup Parmesan cheese, grated

MELT 1 tablespoon of the butter in a large skillet over medium-high heat. Add the onion and mushrooms and sauté until soft, 4 to 5 minutes. Stir in the spinach and basil. Season with salt and pepper. Remove from heat and cool to room temperature.

In a large bowl, beat eggs well with a whisk. Add the half-and-half and season with salt and pepper. Grease a 9 × 13-inch baking dish. Line the bottom of the dish with half of the focaccia pieces to fit snugly (place cut side up). Spread the vegetable mixture over the focaccia and top with the cheeses. Pour the egg mixture over all. Top with remaining focaccia, pressing pieces gently into the egg mixture. Dot top with remaining butter. Cover and refrigerate overnight or for at least 2 hours.

Preheat oven to 350°F. Place the baking dish in a larger roasting pan and fill the pan with hot water until it reaches halfway up the baking dish. Bake until browned on top, about 50 to 60 minutes. Let stand for 5 minutes before cutting, to allow the strata to set.

Chervil Egg Scramble with Chanterelles and Truffle Buttered Toast

Chervil, chanterelles, and truffles are not very common ingredients, and the combination of these three is second to none. Truffles are underground mushrooms that commonly grow near large oak trees. Rare and exotic, some varieties can cost more than $1,000 a pound. For this recipe, the best is not required, and a small can or jar can be found at a specialty grocer or gourmet shop for a reasonable price. If you cannot find truffles, substitute truffle oil: mix in 1 teaspoon with the softened butter.

SERVES 2

½	ounce black truffles
4	tablespoons (½ stick) salted butter, softened
¼	pound fresh chanterelle mushrooms, blemishes removed, sliced
6	large eggs
½	cup whole milk
	Salt and freshly ground black pepper, to taste
2	tablespoons fresh chervil, chopped
4	slices 10-inch boule Sourdough Bread (page 74)

PREHEAT oven or grill to 400°F. Thinly shave the truffles and gently fold into 2 tablespoons butter. Let the butter sit 1 hour or more to infuse it with the truffle flavor.

In a medium or large sauté pan, heat the remaining butter and sauté the mushrooms for about 3 to 5 minutes over medium-high heat, until most of their juices have cooked out.

Beat the eggs in a mixing bowl with the milk and season with salt and pepper. Pour the eggs over the mushrooms and turn the heat to low, stirring occasionally. Cook to desired doneness, about 3 to 4 minutes for wet (partially uncooked) or 5 to 6 minutes for dry (thoroughly cooked). Lightly fold chervil into eggs.

Meanwhile, toast the bread on baking sheets in the oven until golden brown, about 5 minutes per side. Spread with the truffle butter, and serve.

Fennel and Porcini Quiche
with Preserved Lemon

*Most other wild mushrooms, such as oyster, portobello, or crimini, will also work
for this dish. If you can only find dried porcini, use only 2 ounces and rehydrate
in hot water for 20 minutes. Sautéing the rehydrated mushrooms is not necessary.
Preserved lemons can be found at most gourmet and Middle Eastern grocers.*

SERVES 4

1	fennel bulb, trimmed of stalk, leaves reserved for garnish
2	tablespoons extra-virgin olive oil
	Salt and freshly ground black pepper, to taste
½	pound porcini mushrooms, thinly sliced
1½	cups whole milk
4	slices Country White Bread (page 48), crusts removed
8	eggs
½	preserved lemon, thinly sliced, for garnish

PREHEAT oven to 350°F. Thinly slice the fennel and toss with 1 tablespoon of the oil. Season with salt and pepper. Transfer to a shallow baking dish and roast for 20 minutes. In a medium ovenproof sauté pan, heat
the remaining oil until it shimmers. Sauté the mushrooms with salt and
pepper to taste over medium-high heat until most of the water has
cooked out, 5 to 7 minutes. Remove from pan, but do not clean the pan
because this is also going to be your baking dish.

Pour 1 cup of the milk into a wide shallow dish and dip the bread in the
milk. Layer the bread on the bottom of the sauté pan. In a small mixing
bowl, whisk the eggs and remaining milk. Season with salt and pepper.
Stir in the fennel and mushrooms. Pour the mixture over the bread and
bake for 45 minutes. Finish with a garnish of sliced preserved lemon and
fennel leaves and serve.

Chorizo, Egg, and Manchego Stuffed Baguette

This dish served with fresh café con leche *and a glass of Valencia orange juice just may convince you that you're in the outskirts of Madrid.*

SERVES 4

1	baguette, sliced into 4 pieces, each about 4 inches thick
1	tablespoon extra-virgin olive oil
1	small yellow onion, diced
4	ounces Spanish chorizo, thinly sliced
6	large eggs, beaten
¼	cup fresh cilantro or Italian parsley leaves, loosely packed
3	dashes Tabasco sauce
	Salt and freshly ground black pepper, to taste
4	ounces Manchego cheese, thinly sliced

PREHEAT the oven to 450°F. Pull the insides out of the baguette pieces, leaving the crust whole and hollow. Tear the extracted bread into bite-size chunks and set aside.

Heat oil in a medium frying pan over medium-high heat and sauté the onion with the chorizo for about 1 minute. Add the eggs, reserved bread, cilantro, and Tabasco sauce. Season with salt and pepper. Sauté for about 1 minute or until the eggs are almost set. Remove from heat and fold in the cheese.

Using a tablespoon, stuff the baguette pieces with the scramble. Wrap tightly with aluminum foil or parchment paper and bake for 5 to 10 minutes. Remove from the oven, and unwrap carefully to avoid steam burns.

Eggs Benedict with Crab on Ciabatta

SERVES 4

8	eggs
2	loaves ciabatta, cut in half lengthwise and toasted
	Unsalted butter, to taste
12	ounces fresh crabmeat, cooked
½	cup Quick Hollandaise Sauce (recipe follows)
4	teaspoons fresh chives, finely chopped
4	lemon wedges

POUR water into a large skillet or pot to a depth of about 2 inches and bring to a boil. Break an egg into a cup, then carefully slide the egg from the cup into the boiling water. Repeat with the remaining eggs. Immediately reduce the heat so the water barely moves. Cook for about 4 minutes, or until the yolks are still runny but the whites are firm. To test, lift an egg out of the water with a slotted spoon and gently press the thickest part of the white with a finger. If it feels firm to the touch, it's done. Drain.

Butter the toasted ciabatta to taste. Spread a quarter of the crabmeat over each half of the ciabatta loaf. Gently place 2 poached eggs on top of the crabmeat on each ciabatta half. Drizzle about 1 tablespoon of hollandaise sauce over the eggs. Sprinkle 1 teaspoon chives over the sauce and serve immediately with a bowl of the remaining hollandaise sauce and fresh lemon wedges.

Quick Hollandaise Sauce

2   large egg yolks
2   tablespoons boiling water
1   cup (2 sticks) butter, melted and hot
2   tablespoons lemon juice
1   teaspoon fresh herbs, such as parsley, thyme, and basil, minced
    (optional)
    Salt and freshly ground black pepper, to taste

PLACE egg yolks in a blender. Blend at low speed for about 1 minute until pale yellow. While the motor is running, slowly add the boiling water, followed by the hot butter. The butter should be added very slowly, in the thinnest stream possible. When the butter is completely incorporated, add the lemon juice and herbs. Season with salt and pepper. If the sauce is too thick, add a few drops of boiling water. The sauce will hold as you poach the eggs and prepare the other ingredients.

Creamed Wild Mushroom on Ciabatta Toast

Fresh mushrooms are best for this but dried will also work well. Substitute 1 ounce of dried mushrooms for every 4 ounces of fresh. Because of its ability to absorb flavors and liquid, ciabatta is the perfect bread for this dish. It is often used as a bread for dipping. The size of the loaf makes for a perfect edible serving dish.

SERVES 4

1	large loaf ciabatta
2	tablespoons (¼ stick) salted butter
1	tablespoon shallot, minced
1	tablespoon garlic, minced
4	ounces fresh black trumpet mushrooms, well cleaned, cut in half
4	ounces fresh morel mushrooms, well cleaned, cut in half
4	ounces fresh crimini mushrooms, thinly sliced
	Salt and freshly ground black pepper, to taste
2	cups heavy cream
2	tablespoons fresh tarragon, chopped

PREHEAT oven or grill to 400°F. Slice ciabatta in ½-inch sections and toast on baking sheets in the oven, or grill, until golden brown, about 5 minutes per side. The bread should be a little crunchy, but not hard.

Melt the butter over high heat in a large sauté pan and sauté the shallot and garlic until lightly browned, about 1 to 2 minutes. Add the mushrooms and season with salt and pepper. Cook for about 4 to 7 minutes, until most of the juices are cooked out. Add the cream and deglaze. Cook for 3 to 5 minutes until cream has thickened, stirring periodically. Taste and adjust seasoning. If the mixture is too thick, add a little milk. Just before serving stir in the tarragon and spoon over the toasted bread.

Eggs Goldenrod with Hot Hungarian Paprika

To lighten this hearty breakfast dish, you may substitute chicken stock or milk for the half-and-half.

SERVES 4

8	large eggs
2	tablespoons extra-virgin olive oil
2	tablespoons all-purpose flour
2	cups half-and-half
	Salt and freshly ground black pepper, to taste
8	slices Country White Bread (page 48), Rye Bread (page 64), or multi-grain loaf, ½ inch thick and buttered and toasted
2	teaspoons hot Hungarian paprika
8	fresh chives, cut into matchsticks

FILL medium saucepan with cold water, add the eggs, and bring to a boil over high heat. Cover the pan and boil the eggs for 5 minutes, then turn off the heat and leave the pan, covered, on the burner for an additional 5 minutes. Transfer the cooked eggs to an ice bath to speed cooling. Peel and separate the yolks from the whites. Finely dice the whites and chop the yolks, keeping them separated.

In a medium saucepan, whisk oil and flour and cook for 1 minute over medium heat. Add the half-and-half and stir until a smooth sauce is achieved. Add egg whites to the sauce, season with salt and pepper, and serve over toast sprinkled with paprika, chives, and yolks.

Fried Egg Sandwich with Parmigiano-Reggiano and Crimini Mushrooms on Sourdough

Our favorite way to do this sandwich is to only partially cook the egg yolk so when you bite into the sandwich, the yolk oozes out over the cheese, mushrooms, and bread.

SERVES 1

4	tablespoons (½ stick) salted butter
3	large crimini mushrooms, thinly sliced
	Salt and freshly ground black pepper, to taste
2	large eggs
2	slices Sourdough Bread (page 74), toasted
¼	cup Parmigiano-Reggiano cheese, grated, loosely packed

IN A MEDIUM SAUTÉ PAN over medium-high heat, heat 2 tablespoons of the butter. Sauté the sliced mushrooms with salt and pepper for about 3 to 5 minutes, until most of the liquid has cooked out. Remove from pan and wipe clean.

In the same sauté pan, heat the remaining butter over medium-high heat and crack both eggs into the hot pan, being careful not to break the yolks. Season with salt and pepper. When the egg whites begin to turn opaque and bubble on the sides, gently flip the eggs over. Cook for 1 to 2 minutes longer. Top one slice of toast with the eggs, sautéed mushrooms, and grated cheese. Top with the other slice of bread and enjoy.

Sunflower Seed Bread Granola with Apricots

MAKES ABOUT 6 CUPS

2	cups rolled oats
2	cups coarse sunflower seed bread crumbs
1	tablespoon ground cinnamon
1	cup almonds, blanched and sliced (preferably Marcona, a Spanish type of almond with an intense flavor that is wider and flatter than American varieties)
8	tablespoons (1 stick) unsalted butter or ½ cup canola oil
½	cup honey or maple syrup
½	cup light brown sugar, packed
	Zest and juice of 1 large orange
½	teaspoon salt
1	cup dried apricots, coarsely chopped

PREHEAT oven to 375°F. Combine oats, bread crumbs, cinnamon, and almonds in a large bowl. Set aside.

In a medium saucepan over high heat, bring the butter, honey, brown sugar, orange zest, juice, and salt just to a boil. Pour over oat mixture and toss to combine. Spread mixture evenly across a large sheet pan, and bake 25 to 30 minutes, stirring granola occasionally to brown it evenly. Toss the apricots with the warm granola, cool, and store in an airtight container. The granola will keep up to 2 months.

INTERNATIONAL BREAD BITE: JAPAN

Bread was introduced to the people of Japan in the sixteenth century by the Portuguese, but because of the dependence on rice as the staple food of the country, it never caught on. In fact, until the mid-1940s, bread was almost unknown to many Japanese, unless they traveled outside the country. But under the influence of American and European visitors in the later part of the twentieth century, the Japanese people adapted quickly to a new baking philosophy and began to closely mimic the breads of England and France with their own local twist. One Japanese favorite is a soft white bread with a light crust that is filled with bean paste.

With their deepening appreciaton of this timeless art, the Japanese are now considered to be some of the best bakers in the world—and they have the awards to prove it. Held every three years, Le Coupe du Monde is considered the Olympics of baking. It is an intense nine-hour competition featuring teams from twelve countries that are required to produce baked goods in three categories: baguettes and specialty breads; Viennoiserie (Danish pastries); and artistic design, with showpieces made entirely of bread. In 2002 the Japanese team defeated the reigning champions from the United States and a strong French team to capture the crown. They swayed the judges with an innovative green-tea brioche with a uniquely Japanese sweet bean filling.

Grilled Sesame Bagel with Seared Tuna, Daikon Sprouts, and Wasabi Cream Cheese

Daikon sprouts, which can be found at most Asian markets, add some spice to this sandwich.

SERVES 6

FOR THE TUNA

1   pound tuna loin, yellowfin, or other impeccably fresh tuna
1   tablespoon sesame oil
     Salt and freshly ground black pepper, to taste

FOR THE WASABI CREAM CHEESE

¼   cup wasabi powder
¼   cup water
8   ounces cream cheese, softened

6   sesame bagels, halved, buttered, and grilled (or broiled)
1   cup daikon sprouts, loosely packed
2   tablespoons pickled ginger

TO MAKE THE TUNA, heat a large sauté pan over high heat to just before smoking. Rub the tuna loin with sesame oil and season well with salt and pepper. Sear all sides for 1 minute per side. Cut the loin into thin slices against the grain.

FOR THE CREAM CHEESE, in a medium bowl, make a paste with the wasabi and water. Blend evenly with the cream cheese. Spread over the grilled bagel halves and top with tuna and daikon sprouts. Garnish with pickled ginger.

Cinnamon Toast Cereal

MAKES ABOUT 6 CUPS

8	tablespoons (1 stick) unsalted butter
1	teaspoon vanilla extract
1	10-inch boule Sourdough Bread (page 74) or Country White Bread (page 48), crusts removed and cut into cubes about ¼ inch thick and ½ inch wide
¾	cup sugar
3	tablespoons ground cinnamon
½	teaspoon salt

PREHEAT oven to 375°F. In a large stock pot, melt butter over medium-high heat. Add the vanilla extract. Remove from heat and add the bread cubes. Toss to coat evenly with the butter. In a small bowl, combine the sugar, cinnamon, and salt. Set aside. Toss half of the sugar mixture with the bread cubes. Transfer to a baking sheet and bake for 20 to 25 minutes, moving cubes around occasionally to brown evenly. Toss remaining sugar mixture with finished bread. Cool and store in airtight container.

Three-Cheese Bread
(page 54)

Chanterelle and Shallot Bruschetta (page 87)

Goat Cheese Tartlets with Caramelized Onions and Figs (page 100)

Sourdough French Toast with Strawberry Rhubarb Jam

(page 145)

Spinach and Roma Tomato Omelet Sandwich on Kalamata Loaf

(page 135)

BLT with Apple-Wood Smoked Bacon, Beefsteak Tomato, Arugula, and
Lemon Aioli on Sourdough (page 150)

Roasted Beet Caprese with Buffalo
Mozzarella and Three-Seed Croutons

(page 194)

Cream of Artichoke Soup with Chervil and Fried Artichokes (page 186)

Salad of Ciabatta, Celeriac, Grapes, Walnuts, and Apple (page 196)

Wild Mushroom Stuffing (page 208)

Blueberry Buttermilk Bread Pudding with Maple Syrup (page 227)

Zinfandel-Poached Pears with
Raisin Pecan Streusel (page 237)

Chocolate Panini (page 247)

Individual Raisin Pecan Bread Pudding with Orange Marmalade (page 230)

Sourdough French Bread (page 77)
wih Rye Bread (center, page 64)

One-Eyed Susans with Cured Salmon and Dill Crème Fraîche

SERVES 4

1	cup crème fraîche or good-quality sour cream
¼	cup fresh dill leaves, chopped, packed
	Salt and freshly ground black pepper, to taste
4	slices pumpernickel loaf, ½ inch thick and buttered
4	large eggs
¼	pound Quick Citrus-Cured Salmon (page 106), Quick Pastrami-Cured Salmon (page 108), or smoked salmon slices
	Dill leaves, capers, and minced red onion, for garnish

COMBINE the crème fraîche with the dill. Season with salt and pepper.

With a biscuit or small round cookie cutter, cut rounds out of the center of each slice of bread. Heat a large sauté pan to medium, and place the bread frame and rounds in the pan separately, buttered side down. Toast 1 to 2 minutes; then flip the bread. Crack 1 egg in the center of each bread frame. Cook 2 to 3 minutes. Remove bread rounds. Remove pan from heat, and cover for an additional 2 minutes to finish cooking eggs. Serve each one-eyed Susan with its round, a dollop of crème fraîche, and 2 to 3 slices of salmon, and garnish.

Over Easy Egg with Pancetta on Asiago Loaf

Pancetta is a cured bacon from a pork loin. Robust and salty, this variety has less fat than traditional bacon with a meatier flavor. Unlike bacon, pancetta does not come in strips but rather in a sausagelike roll. If pancetta cannot be found, high-quality bacon is an alternative. Prosciutto also works, but should not be cooked.

SERVES 2

2   tablespoons (¼ stick) salted butter
4   slices Three-Cheese Bread (page 54) or Panera Bread Asiago Cheese, 1 inch thick
4   teaspoons olive oil
4   slices pancetta
4   eggs
Salt and freshly ground black pepper, to taste

PREHEAT oven or grill to 400°F. Spread 1 tablespoon butter on the bread. Toast on baking sheets in the oven, or grill, until golden brown, about 5 minutes per side.

In a small sauté pan, heat the oil over medium heat until it shimmers. If the meat is very fatty, the oil is not necessary. Cook the pancetta until it starts to brown, about 5 minutes. A little crispiness is good, but overcooking will make it rubbery. After the pancetta is cooked, place it on a paper towel to drain.

In the same sauté pan, melt the remaining butter on high heat. Crack eggs into the pan, season with salt and pepper, and cook until egg whites have turned white. Then flip the eggs and cook another 10 to 15 seconds. The yolks should still be runny. Place two eggs on each of two toasted bread slices, then place two slices of pancetta on eggs, and top with the other slices of bread.

Kitchen Sink Brunch Casserole

We call this the Kitchen Sink Casserole because it's perfect for getting rid of left-overs. Chopped broccoli, tomatoes, peppers, mushrooms, or whatever's in the fridge can add a new flavor each time you make it.

SERVES 4–6

2	tablespoons (¼ stick) butter, softened
6–8	slices French bread or Sourdough Bread (page 74), cut into ½-inch cubes
1	pound bacon, cooked and crumbled
⅓	cup spinach, cooked, chopped, and well drained
1½	cups Cheddar cheese, shredded
5	large eggs, beaten
2	cups half-and-half
1	teaspoon salt
1	teaspoon dried mustard
3	scallions (white and green parts), chopped, for garnish
1	tablespoon fresh parsley, chopped, for garnish

BUTTER a 13 × 9-inch baking pan. Place bread cubes in baking pan. Add bacon and spinach. Top with cheese. Whisk together eggs, half-and-half, salt, and dried mustard. Pour over bread mixture, covering thoroughly. Cover baking pan with plastic wrap and refrigerate overnight.

Preheat oven to 350°F. Remove plastic wrap and bake for 35 to 45 minutes, or until set and browned on top. Garnish with scallions and parsley.

Poached Eggs with Country Ham and Red-Eye Gravy

SERVES 4

4   slices country ham steak (about ½ pound), ¼ inch thick
1   tablespoon all-purpose flour
1   cup strong-brewed black coffee
    Salt and freshly ground black pepper, to taste
2   tablespoons lemon juice or white wine vinegar
    Salt and freshly ground black pepper, to taste
8   large eggs
8   slices Sourdough Bread (page 74), ½ inch thick, toasted, and
    buttered

IN A SAUTÉ PAN over medium-high heat, sear the ham steaks 2 to 3 minutes per side and remove from pan. Whisk the flour into the pan drippings and cook for 1 minute. Add the coffee, and bring to a boil. Remove from heat and season with salt and pepper. Keep warm until ready to use.

In a large saucepan, bring 2 inches of water, the lemon juice, and salt to taste to a boil. Reduce heat to just below boiling. Crack eggs and gently drop into the water one at a time. Poach for 2 minutes for runny yolks and 3 minutes for a firmer yolk. Serve over toasted bread with ham steaks and plenty of gravy.

Sharlotka with Apples, Pecans, and Raisins

A sharlotka *is a Polish bread pudding that is made from a darker, heartier loaf of bread. This Slavic dish is typically eaten for breakfast. It differs from the dessert version, or "Charlotte," that is traditionally made with a white or semolina bread as a base.*

SERVES 6–8

4	tablespoons (½ stick) unsalted butter
1	loaf Cinnamon Raisin White Bread (page 50) or Raisin Pecan White Bread (page 51), torn into bite-size pieces
½	cup brown sugar, packed
½	cup pecan halves
	Zest and juice of 1 large orange
¼	cup apple cider
1	tablespoon vanilla extract or rum
8	small baking apples (about 2 pounds) such as Fuji, Gala, or Granny Smith, peeled, cored, and thinly sliced
½	cup apple, quince, or blackberry jam or jelly

PREHEAT oven to 400°F. Melt the butter in a medium saucepan over medium heat. Add the bread and cook for 2 to 3 minutes, or until well coated. Add the sugar, pecans, orange zest and juice, cider, and vanilla extract. Cook an additional 2 to 3 minutes until a sauce begins to form.

In a 9 × 13-inch baking dish, layer the bread mixture with the apples, and dot the top with the jam or jelly. Bake 30 to 40 minutes, or until bubbly.

Soft-Boiled Egg with Focaccia Sticks and Eggplant "Caviar"

SERVES 4

½ pan Focaccia Bread (page 53) sliced into strips about 3 inches long, ¼ inch thick, and ½ inch wide
2–3 tablespoons extra-virgin olive oil
4 large eggs
Eggplant "Caviar" (see Spicy Chickpea Fritters with Eggplant "Caviar," page 110)
Salt and freshly ground black pepper, to taste

PREHEAT oven or grill to 400°F. Toss focaccia with the oil, then toast on a baking sheet in the oven, or grill, until golden brown, about 5 minutes per side.

Place eggs in a medium saucepan and cover with cold water. Bring to a boil. Remove the eggs after they have boiled for 2 minutes. Place each egg in a shot glass, crack off the tops, and add 1 teaspoon of the eggplant caviar to each egg. Serve the focaccia sticks on the side for dipping.

Spinach and Roma Tomato Omelet Sandwich on Kalamata Loaf

This dish can also be served as a brunch frittata, with Kalamata Olive Bread croutons, instead of as a sandwich.

SERVES 1

2	teaspoons salted butter
2	slices Kalamata Olive Bread (page 52)
1	tablespoon olive oil
1	teaspoon garlic, minced
1	small Roma tomato, cored and cut into ¼-inch dice
15	spinach leaves, stemmed
	Salt and freshly ground black pepper, to taste
2	large eggs, beaten
1	tablespoon Parmigiano-Reggiano cheese, grated (optional)

PREHEAT oven or grill to 400°F. Spread the butter on each slice of bread and toast on baking sheets in the oven, or grill, until golden brown, about 5 minutes per side.

In an omelet pan or small sauté pan, heat the oil over medium heat until it shimmers. Sauté the garlic until it turns light brown and then add the tomato and spinach. Season with salt and pepper. Cook spinach for 1 to 2 minutes, until wilted a little but not totally limp. Add the eggs and cook until they are solid enough to flip, about 2 to 3 minutes. Once flipped, add the cheese and cook for 30 seconds to 1 minute more. Place omelet on toasted bread. Slice and top with other slice.

Vegetable Garden Frittata

SERVES 8

8	tablespoons (1 stick) unsalted butter
1	teaspoon garlic, minced
1	cup asparagus tips
1	cup broccoli florets, steamed
1	cup Roma tomatoes, chopped
2	cups sourdough bread crumbs
2	teaspoons Italian seasoning
10	large eggs, lightly beaten
1	cup Cheddar cheese, grated
	Salt and freshly ground black pepper, to taste

PREHEAT oven to 350°F. In a skillet, melt 4 tablespoons of the butter. Add the garlic, asparagus, broccoli, and tomatoes and cook for 2 minutes. Add bread crumbs and Italian seasoning and cook for an additional 2 minutes. Set aside. In a separate ovenproof non-stick skillet, melt the remaining butter over medium heat. Add the eggs and let them cook for 2 minutes. When the eggs begin to solidify, add the vegetable–bread crumb mixture and cheese. Stir gently without disturbing the bottom portion of the pan. Transfer the pan to the oven and bake for 10 minutes. Remove from oven and invert frittata onto a serving plate. Serve by cutting into wedges or squares.

Welsh Rarebit with Belgian Ale and White Cheddar

SERVES 6

2	tablespoons (¼ stick) butter
2	tablespoons all-purpose flour
12	ounces Belgian white ale
1	teaspoon Worcestershire sauce
1	teaspoon Tabasco sauce
1	teaspoon Dijon mustard
2	cups white Cheddar cheese, shredded
	Salt and freshly ground black pepper, to taste
12	slices Country White Bread (page 48), ½ inch thick and toasted
	Fresh chives, for garnish

MELT the butter in a medium saucepan over low heat. Whisk in the flour and cook for 1 minute. Whisk in ale, Worcestershire sauce, Tabasco sauce, mustard, and cheese. Season with salt and pepper. Stir over low heat until a smooth sauce is formed. Serve the sauce over toasted bread and garnish with chives.

Deviled Chile Crab with Thai Basil

This dish is the perfect focal point for any spring or summer brunch. The deviled chile crab will transport your taste buds to the Eastern shore of Maryland, while the Thai basil will offer flavors of the orient.

SERVES 6

6	live Blue or Dungeness crabs
1	bird or serrano chile, seeded and minced
1	tablespoon hot Hungarian or Spanish paprika
1	tablespoon dried mustard
1	tablespoon Tabasco sauce
1	teaspoon soy sauce
1	cup heavy cream
4	hard-boiled eggs, minced
2	cups sourdough bread crumbs
½	cup fresh Thai basil, chopped
	Salt and freshly ground black pepper, to taste
	Olive oil, for drizzling

PREHEAT oven to 400°F. Place the crabs in a large pot of boiling, salted water and cook them until all are bright red, about 3 to 5 minutes. Remove and cool. Remove the top shell from the crabs, keeping it intact. Rinse and reserve. Pick out all the meat, from claws, legs, and behind the head, discarding the gills. Set the picked meat aside.

In a large bowl, combine the chile, paprika, dried mustard, Tabasco sauce, soy sauce, cream, eggs, bread crumbs, and all but 2 tablespoons of the basil. Season with salt and pepper. Fill the cavity of each crab top-shell with the stuffing and bake on a sheet pan, stuffing side up, for 20 to 25 minutes, or until a crust begins to form. Serve with a drizzle of the oil and a sprinkle of the reserved basil.

Waffle-Grilled Raisin Pecan Sandwich with Honey Mascarpone

SERVES 4

1	cup mascarpone cheese
¼	cup honey
½	teaspoon salt
8	slices Raisin Pecan White Bread (page 51), ½ inch thick and buttered

PREHEAT a waffle iron or grill pan. In a bowl, blend the mascarpone, honey, and salt until smooth. Divide and spread evenly over the unbuttered sides of 4 bread slices, top with remaining 4 slices, and grill with the buttered sides out for 3 minutes, or until golden.

Turkey Pot Pie with Buttermilk–Country White Bread Crust

This quick and satisfying brunch dish will help reduce holiday leftovers, while offering a new twist on a classic.

SERVES 8

CRUST

1   loaf Country White Bread (page 48), crusts removed, sliced ½ inch thick

2   cups buttermilk
   Salt and freshly ground black pepper, to taste

FILLING

2   tablespoons (¼ stick) unsalted butter

2   tablespoons all-purpose flour

2   cups Chicken Stock (page 185)

1   large onion, cut into 1-inch dice

4   ribs celery, sliced ¼ inch thick

4   medium carrots, peeled and sliced, ¼ inch thick

1   tablespoon fresh thyme, coarsely chopped

1   large garlic clove, minced

1   tablespoon extra-virgin olive oil

1   pound roasted turkey meat, shredded

1   cup green beans, cut into 1-inch pieces

PREHEAT oven to 400°F. To make the crust, in a large bowl, soak the bread in the buttermilk, and season with salt and pepper.

TO MAKE THE FILLING, in a medium saucepan, melt the butter over medium heat. Stir in the flour and cook for 1 minute. Whisk in the stock and continue cooking until the sauce thickens, about 2 minutes.

In a sauté pan over medium heat, sweat the onion, celery, carrots, thyme, and garlic in the oil. Season with salt and pepper. Add the turkey and beans and transfer to a 9 × 13-inch baking dish. Pour the sauce over the mixture and carefully top with the soaked bread. Bake 25 to 30 minutes.

Spoonbread with White Cheddar and Chives

A classic breakfast mainstay in the American South, this easy-to-prepare spoon-bread makes any morning meal memorable.

SERVES 8

8   large eggs
2   cups buttermilk
2   cups sour cream
1   teaspoon ground cayenne pepper
    Salt and freshly ground black pepper, to taste
2   cups white Cheddar cheese, shredded
1   small bunch fresh chives, finely chopped
8   cups crustless ½-inch cubes Country White Bread (page 48) or
    Sourdough Bread (page 74)

PREHEAT oven to 400°F. In a large bowl, whisk the eggs, buttermilk, and sour cream until smooth. Season well with cayenne pepper, salt, and black pepper. Fold in the cheese, chives, and bread and transfer to a buttered 9 × 13-inch baking dish. Bake 30 to 35 minutes, or until golden brown on top.

Oven French Toast

SERVES 6–8

6	tablespoons (¾ stick) butter
6–8	slices Cinnamon Raisin White Bread (page 50), 1 inch thick
1	cup pecans, coarsely chopped
½	cup light brown sugar
2	tablespoons dark corn syrup
4	large eggs
1	teaspoon vanilla extract
1½	cups half-and-half
1	cup whole milk
½	teaspoon ground cinnamon
1	dash ground nutmeg

PREHEAT oven to 350°F. Generously butter a 13 × 9-inch baking pan. Butter both sides of bread and place in the baking pan, covering the bottom of the pan. In a small bowl, toss the pecans with the brown sugar and distribute over the bread. Drizzle corn syrup over pecans. In a medium bowl, whisk together eggs, vanilla extract, half-and-half, milk, cinnamon, and nutmeg. Pour evenly over bread slices. Set aside for 15 to 30 minutes to allow the bread to absorb the liquid. Bake for 30 to 45 minutes, until brown. Invert on a serving tray, cut into squares, and enjoy piping hot.

Overnight Eggnog French Toast

This festive version of an old breakfast standby is assembled the night before, so the only work to do on a busy holiday morning is baking it.

SERVES 6–8

4	cups eggnog
4	large eggs
1	teaspoon ground cinnamon
½	teaspoon ground nutmeg
½	teaspoon vanilla extract
16	slices Sourdough Bread (page 74), ½ inch thick
4	tablespoons (½ stick) unsalted butter, melted
	Confectioners' sugar, for dusting
	Fresh fruit or fruit compote (optional)

Whisk together eggnog, eggs, cinnamon, nutmeg, and vanilla extract in a large bowl. Arrange the bread slices in a single layer in two 9 × 13-inch glass or ceramic baking pans. Pour the eggnog mixture over the bread to cover all slices equally. Cover with foil and refrigerate at least 6 hours or overnight.

PREHEAT oven to 450°F. Brush two large rimmed baking sheets with the butter. Carefully transfer the bread slices to the baking sheets using a spatula. Brush the tops of the bread with the remaining melted butter. Bake the bread for 10 minutes, or until lightly golden on one side. Flip the slices and bake until golden brown and crisp on the outside, about 6 minutes more. Serve with a dusting of confectioners' sugar and top with fresh fruit, fruit compote, or your favorite syrup or preserve.

Bananas Foster French Toast

A New Orleans–inspired dish that highlights the nutty, slightly sweet flavor and aroma of the sesame seeds.

SERVES 6

FRENCH TOAST

12	large eggs
3	cups half-and-half
½	cup sugar
1	tablespoon vanilla extract
1	tablespoon ground cinnamon
	Zest of 1 orange or lemon
1	teaspoon salt
12	slices sesame seed bread, such as Panera Bread Sesame Semolina, ½ inch thick
¼	cup canola or olive oil

BANANAS FOSTER

4	tablespoons (½ stick) unsalted butter
4	large, ripe bananas, peeled and cut into ½-inch slices
½	cup brown sugar, packed
¼	cup dark rum
1	tablespoon ground cinnamon

TO MAKE THE FRENCH TOAST, combine the eggs, half-and-half, sugar, vanilla extract, cinnamon, zest, and salt in a large shallow bowl. Dip the bread in the egg mixture and coat evenly. Heat a large sauté pan over medium heat. Add the oil and fry the egg-soaked bread for 2 to 3 minutes per side until golden brown.

FOR THE BANANAS FOSTER, heat a separate pan over high heat. Melt the butter. Sauté the bananas with the butter and sugar. Deglaze with the rum and *carefully* flambé by igniting. After the flame goes out, sprinkle the cinnamon over the mixture. Serve the bananas over French toast.

Sourdough French Toast with Strawberry Rhubarb Jam

SERVES 6

12	large eggs
3	cups half-and-half
1	tablespoon vanilla extract
1	tablespoon ground cinnamon
½	cup sugar
	Zest of 1 orange or lemon
1	teaspoon salt
12	slices Sourdough Bread (page 74), ½ inch thick
4	tablespoons canola or olive oil
	Confectioners' sugar, for dusting
	Unsalted butter
1	cup Strawberry Rhubarb Jam (recipe follows)

COMBINE eggs, half-and-half, vanilla extract, cinnamon, sugar, zest, and salt in a large shallow bowl. Dip the bread in the egg mixture and coat evenly. Heat a large sauté pan over medium heat, add the oil, and fry the bread for 2 to 3 minutes per side. Dust with confectioners' sugar and serve with the butter and Strawberry Rhubarb Jam.

Strawberry Rhubarb Jam

MAKES 1 PINT

2	pints ripe strawberries, hulled and quartered
4	large stalks rhubarb, trimmed and cut into ¼-inch slices
2	cups sugar
1	cup water

BRING all of the ingredients to a boil in medium saucepan, reduce to low heat, and simmer 30 to 40 minutes, stirring occasionally. Cool and store in an airtight container. This will keep for up to 1 month in the refrigerator.

Sandwiches

The rising popularity of artisan bread has had an incredible impact on this traditional and versatile bread-based dish. A simple assembly of lunch meats and cheeses has extended into the exotic. Plastic-bagged loaves on the grocery shelf just can't host the sophisticated pairings of today's gourmet sandwiches.

From lamb loin and mint yogurt, to goat cheese and Thai basil, gourmet sandwiches require breads with a character and texture to support the unique marriage of extraordinary ingredients. Yet even classic combinations are trading up to artisan. Gooey grilled cheese and peanut butter and jelly are rising to new heights between two rustic slices, proving that both the simple and extravagant are better with artisan bread.

Mediterranean Veggie Sandwich

SERVES 1

3	tablespoons olive oil or butter, plus extra for the bell pepper
1	large onion, sliced into ⅛-inch-thick rings
1	pinch salt
1	pinch freshly ground black pepper
1	pinch sugar
1	red bell pepper
3	tablespoons garlic-flavored hummus
2	slices sunflower seed bread, such as Panera Bread Sunflower Seed
1	leaf romaine lettuce
3–4	slices vine-ripened tomato, ¼ inch thick
4	slices cucumber, ⅛ inch thick
1	tablespoon feta cheese, crumbled

IN A LARGE NON-STICK SKILLET over medium-high heat, heat 3 tablespoons of the oil. Add the onion and stir until it is thoroughly coated with the oil. Add the salt, black pepper, and sugar and continue to stir. As the onion cooks, it may stick to the bottom of the pan. Deglaze with small amounts of hot water, one teaspoon at a time. Continue to stir until the onion is soft and a deep golden brown. Remove from the heat and put aside 5 to 8 rings for the sandwich. Reserve the remaining caramelized onion for another use.

Roast the red pepper: Preheat the oven to broil. Lightly brush the pepper with olive oil and place on a pan under the broiler 4 to 5 inches below the heat source. Carefully watch the pepper and turn as each side begins to char slightly. Once the pepper is fully roasted (all sides have a flaky, charred appearance), remove it from the oven, place it in a bowl, and cover with plastic wrap for 15 minutes. This will allow the pepper to continue to cook while the skin loosens.

Remove the plastic wrap and run the pepper under cold water to cool. Peel the skin away from the pepper. Cut off the top of the pepper and remove all the seeds and membranes. Slice the pepper into strips, about 3 inches long and 1 inch wide. Put aside 3 slices of the roasted pepper for the sandwich. Reserve the rest for another use.

To make the sandwich, spread the hummus in a thin layer over one side of each bread slice to cover end to end. On top of one slice, layer lettuce, tomato, onion, cucumber, and roasted pepper. Sprinkle cheese evenly across the top. Top with second bread slice and serve.

BLT with Apple-Wood Smoked Bacon, Beefsteak Tomato, Arugula, and Lemon Aioli on Sourdough

SERVES 2

1	tablespoon unsalted butter
4	slices Sourdough Bread (page 74)
8	slices apple-wood smoked bacon
¼	cup mayonnaise
2	tablespoons fresh lemon juice
	Salt and freshly ground black pepper, to taste
4	slices beefsteak tomato
1	cup arugula, lightly packed

SPREAD butter on one side of all 4 slices of bread and toast until golden brown. In a medium cast-iron pan or other heavy sauté pan, cook the bacon over medium heat until it is crispy, 6 to 8 minutes. Drain on a paper towel.

To make the aioli, whisk the mayonnaise and lemon juice together and season with salt and pepper. Spread the aioli on the buttered side of the bread slices, and top with the bacon, tomato, and arugula. Finish with the remaining slices of bread, slice each sandwich in half, and serve.

Grilled Lamb Loin on Focaccia with Roasted Tomato and Mint Yogurt Sauce

SERVES 4

1	pound lamb loin
¼	cup + 3 tablespoons extra-virgin olive oil
	Salt and freshly ground black pepper, to taste
4	Roma tomatoes, cored and sliced in half lengthwise
2	teaspoons garlic, minced
½	cup whole-milk yogurt
2	tablespoons fresh mint, chiffonade
1	tablespoon apple cider vinegar
1	tablespoon sugar
4	loaves rosemary Focaccia Bread (page 53), cut into 3-inch squares and halved widthwise

PREHEAT oven to 400°F. Separately, preheat a grill to 400°F. Rub ¼ cup oil over the lamb loin, place in between two pieces of plastic wrap, and pound with a mallet to a 1 inch thickness. Season the lamb with salt and pepper. Oil the grill with 1 tablespoon olive oil and cook the meat for 3 to 4 minutes per side to get a medium doneness. Cook longer if you prefer well-done meat. Remove the meat from heat and let it rest for 10 minutes. Thinly slice against the grain at a 45-degree angle.

Toss the tomatoes with 1 tablespoon oil and the garlic. Season with salt and pepper. Roast the tomatoes in a roasting pan in the oven for 25 to 30 minutes.

In a small bowl, mix the yogurt, mint, vinegar, and sugar. Season with salt and pepper.

Lightly brush the remaining tablespoon of the oil on the cut sides of the bread. Toast on a baking sheet in the oven or grill until golden brown, about 5 minutes per side. Evenly layer the lamb on the grilled bread. Top with the roasted tomatoes, yogurt sauce, and top slice of focaccia.

Tuscan Chicken Sandwich

SERVES 1

2   tablespoons Panera Bread Balsamic Vinaigrette (recipe follows)

½   loaf rosemary Focaccia Bread (page 53), cut horizontally to create a top and bottom

1   cup mixed field greens, loosely packed

3–4   slices vine-ripened tomato, ¼ inch thick

3–4   slices red onion, ¼ inch thick

3   ounces boneless, skinless chicken breast, grilled and sliced thinly on a bias

1   tablespoon mayonnaise

1   tablespoon basil pesto (high-quality, store bought)

SPREAD Balsamic Vinaigrette in a thin layer over one side of one bread slice to cover end to end. On top of the vinaigrette, layer greens, tomato, onion, and chicken. Combine mayonnaise and pesto in a small bowl. Spread pesto mayonnaise on remaining slice of bread. Top sandwich and serve.

Panera Bread Balsamic Vinaigrette

MAKES ABOUT 4½ CUPS

1   cup balsamic vinegar

2   tablespoons fresh basil, chiffonade

2   tablespoons fresh tarragon, chiffonade

2   tablespoons fresh oregano, finely chopped

2   tablespoons fresh chives, finely chopped

2   garlic cloves, minced
     Salt and freshly ground black pepper, to taste

3   cups extra-virgin olive oil

COMBINE all ingredients in medium mixing bowl except olive oil. Mix well with wire whisk, and then slowly pour in the olive oil while continuing to whisk to form an emulsion.

Pork Loin Baguette with Gruyère, Watercress, and Fig Jam

SERVES 2

¾   pound pork loin
¼   cup olive oil
    Salt and freshly ground black pepper, to taste
1   medium baguette, halved lengthwise
4   ounces Gruyère cheese, thinly sliced or grated
    Fig Jam (recipe follows)
1   cup watercress, stems removed

PREHEAT oven to 350°F. Rub the pork with oil and season with salt and pepper. Roast for 20 to 25 minutes, or until internal temperature of pork reaches 155°F. Remove from heat and allow the meat to rest for 10 minutes. Slice the pork thinly against the grain.

Increase the oven temperature to 400°F. Toast the bread on baking sheets in the oven until golden brown, about 5 minutes per side. Place cheese on bread and toast for 3 to 5 additional minutes, or until the cheese is melted.

Spread the Fig Jam on the bread, then top with the pork and watercress.

Fig Jam

MAKES 1 PINT

2   pints figs, halved pole to pole
1   cup sugar
½   cup water
1   pinch salt

IN A MEDIUM SAUCEPAN, combine all of the ingredients. Cook over medium-low heat for 10 to 15 minutes. Mash with a fork to form a chunky paste. Cool and store in an airtight container.

BBQ Tofu with Pickled Radishes

SERVES 4

BBQ SAUCE

1	small yellow onion, diced
1	large garlic clove, minced
1	28-ounce can whole, peeled tomatoes (organic plum or San Marzano) or 6 ripe Roma tomatoes, peeled
½	cup apple cider vinegar
½	cup molasses
2	tablespoons Worcestershire sauce
2	tablespoons Tabasco sauce
	Salt and freshly ground black pepper, to taste

PICKLED RADISH

1	cup water
1	cup apple cider vinegar
½	cup sugar
¼	cup salt
12	red radishes, sliced top to bottom, ¼ inch thick

1	pound firm tofu, sliced lengthwise into 4 slabs
8	slices of sesame seed bread, such as Panera Bread Sesame Semolina, ½ inch thick, toasted and buttered

TO PREPARE THE BBQ SAUCE, sweat the onion and garlic in a medium saucepan over medium heat for 1 to 2 minutes. Add the tomatoes, vinegar, molasses, Worcestershire sauce, and Tabasco sauce. Season with salt and pepper and bring to a boil. Reduce heat to low and simmer 30 to 45 minutes, or until syrupy. Place in a blender, making certain to vent (or else the heat pressure will make a BBQ-sauce bomb), and blend until smooth.

TO PICKLE THE RADISHES, place the radishes in a medium bowl. Bring the water and vinegar to a boil. Completely dissolve the sugar and salt in the boiling mixture. Pour over the radishes, and set aside to cool. Refrigerate until ready to use.

Preheat oven to 400°F. Place the tofu slabs in a medium baking dish. Pour half the BBQ sauce over it, reserving the remaining sauce for a future use. Bake for 45 minutes to 1 hour. Serve the hot tofu on toasted bread with pickled radish slices.

Black-Eyed Pea Burger on Challah

SERVES 6

1	small onion, diced
1	large garlic clove, minced
4	large sprigs fresh thyme, stemmed and coarsely chopped
2	pounds black-eyed peas, cooked, or 1 32-ounce can
1	cup cooked white rice
1	tablespoon Worcestershire sauce
1	tablespoon Tabasco sauce
1	tablespoon Dijon mustard
¼	cup canola or extra-virgin olive oil, plus extra for frying
	Salt and freshly ground black pepper, to taste
¼	cup egg whites (about 4 large eggs)
1	cup sourdough or white bread crumbs
12	slices challah, lightly toasted
	Green leaf lettuce (optional)
	Tomatoes, sliced (optional)
	Kosher pickles (optional)
	Ketchup (optional)
	Dijon mustard (optional)
	Mayonnaise (optional)
	Minced red onion (optional)

SAUTÉ the onion, garlic, and thyme in a large sauté pan over medium heat. Add the onion mixture, black-eyed peas, white rice, Worcestershire sauce, Tabasco sauce, mustard, and oil in the bowl of a food processor. Season with salt and pepper. Add egg whites and bread crumbs. Pulse in the food processor until consistent and cohesive but still somewhat chunky. Roll into 6 balls and form into patties. Fry the patties in oil in a sauté pan over medium heat for about 3 to 4 minutes each side, or until crispy. Serve on toasted challah with desired condiments.

Bacon Turkey Bravo

SERVES 1

2	tablespoons Signature Dressing (recipe follows)
2	slices Panera Bread Tomato Basil
1	leaf romaine lettuce
3–4	slices vine-ripened tomato, ¼ inch thick
4	ounces smoked turkey breast, sliced wafer-thin
1	slice smoked Gouda cheese
2	strips bacon, cooked until crispy

TO MAKE THE SANDWICH, spread the Signature Dressing over one side of one bread slice to cover end to end. On top of the dressing, layer lettuce, tomato, turkey, Gouda, and bacon, crisscrossing the bacon slices. Top with the second slice of bread and serve.

Signature Dressing

MAKES ABOUT 1¾ CUPS

1	cup mayonnaise
½	cup ketchup
2	tablespoons lemon juice, freshly squeezed
½	teaspoon dried mustard
1	teaspoon Worcestershire sauce
1	dash Tabasco sauce (optional)

COMBINE the mayonnaise, ketchup, lemon juice, dried mustard, Worcestershire sauce, and Tabasco sauce in a small bowl. Stir thoroughly until all ingredients are incorporated. Refrigerate in an airtight container.

Chicken Salad Croissant with Horseradish and Lime

This recipe also works with leftover roasted chicken from last night's dinner.

SERVES 4

1	4-pound chicken, cut up
	Salt and freshly ground black pepper, to taste
½	cup extra-virgin olive oil
½	cup mayonnaise
¼	cup fresh cilantro leaves, packed
¾	cup fresh horseradish, peeled, finely grated
¼	cup fresh lime juice
1	teaspoon hot paprika
4	large croissants

PREHEAT oven to 350°F. Rinse the chicken pieces in cold water and pat dry. Season with salt, pepper, and half of the oil. Arrange the chicken pieces in a single layer in a roasting pan. Roast for 20 minutes, remove from oven, and set aside to cool. Once cooled, discard the skin, pull the meat from the bone, and shred.

In medium bowl, whisk together remaining oil, mayonnaise, cilantro, horseradish, lime juice, and paprika. Fold in the shredded chicken and season to taste.

Slice croissants in half lengthwise and toast until golden brown. Spread a quarter of the chicken salad mixture on the bottom half of each croissant, and place other half of croissant on top to finish.

INTERNATIONAL BREAD BITE: FRANCE

The French are known for their bread. They have a passion for fresh-baked baguettes, brioche, and croissants. Unlike many cultures and regions, very few French bake their own bread at home; they prefer to visit their local *boulangerie* on a daily basis. Typically, the French are known for the baguette, but this long, slender loaf with a crispy crust was not developed until the 1930s when new yeasts were developed along with technological advancements in ovens and mechanized kneading. This, together with generations of baking knowledge, led to the popularity of this French bread treasure.

There are many explanations as to why the baguette tastes best when baked and eaten in France. French flours are much softer than North American varieties and lend themselves better to the soft, light crumb. Skillful bakers use small amounts of yeast, combined with long kneading and rising periods, to create bread that has a crisp, thin crust and delicious, soft crumb.

Over the past century French bread has lost considerable ground in terms of consumption and quality. In 1900 each person ate, on average, two pounds of bread per day. Today, the average person in France consumes about 5½ ounces. Changes in diet can account for some of the decline, but some say the industrialization of breadmaking in the country is the real reason. More bread, made faster through technology, has affected the quality, so much that the government has intervened. Recent legislation was introduced to prevent any bakery from calling itself a *boulangerie* if it does not make, knead, and bake entirely from scratch on its premises.

Lobster Roll with Herbed Aioli

Aioli is a light mayonnaise-style sauce laden with fresh garlic and herbs, often used atop vegetables or fish. For this recipe, a quality light mayonnaise can be used for the base and flavored with fresh herbs before serving.

SERVES 2

¾   gallon cold water
2   tablespoons salt, plus more to taste
1   2-pound live lobster
⅓   cup mayonnaise
½   teaspoon fresh tarragon, finely chopped
½   teaspoon fresh chives, finely chopped
½   teaspoon fresh Italian parsley, finely chopped
½   teaspoon fresh thyme leaves, finely chopped
     Freshly ground black pepper, to taste
2   ciabatta rolls

IN A LARGE STOCK POT, bring the water to a boil and add the salt. Drop the lobster into the boiling water and cook for 5 to 6 minutes, or until the lobster is pink all over. Remove from the water and cool. Remove all the meat from the tail and claws and cut meat into a ¼-inch dice. To remove the meat from the claws, use a set of pliers or the back of a chef's knife to crack the claw shell, using a small fork to slide the claw meat out. To remove the meat from the lobster tail, turn the tail shell side down and, using a sharp chef's knife, cut the tail in half. The meat can be easily pulled out by hand.

In a medium bowl, mix together the mayonnaise with the tarragon, chives, parsley, and thyme. Fold in the lobster meat and season with salt and pepper. Cut the ciabatta in half lengthwise. Evenly divide the lobster salad between the rolls. Cut in half and serve.

Curried Egg Salad Croissant with Daikon Sprouts and Roma Tomato

Any sprout can replace the daikon sprouts for this dish, but daikon adds a unique spiciness. Gherkins, shallots, and/or walnuts also make great additions.

SERVES 2

6	large eggs
2	teaspoons curry powder
½	cup mayonnaise
1	tablespoon fresh cilantro, chiffonade
	Salt and freshly ground black pepper, to taste
2	large croissants, halved widthwise
⅔	cup daikon sprouts
1	Roma tomato, seeded and cut into 8 thin slices

BOIL the eggs by covering them in a medium saucepan with cold water and bringing the water to a boil over high heat. Cover the pan and boil the eggs for 5 minutes; then turn off the heat and leave the pan, covered, on the burner for an additional 5 minutes. Transfer the cooked eggs to an ice bath to speed cooling. Peel and roughly chop the eggs. In a medium bowl, use a spatula to gently combine the eggs, curry powder, mayonnaise, and cilantro. Season with salt and pepper. Place half the egg salad on the bottom half of each of the croissants. Top with the sprouts and tomato slices. Finish with the croissant tops and serve.

Grilled Flank Steak and Arugula with Pickled Red Onion and Horseradish Aioli

Any meat needs to rest after it has been cooked to retain its juices. If the meat is cut just after being cooked, the juices will run all over your cutting board, and the meat will be dry.

SERVES 4

1	pound flank steak
¼	cup + 2 tablespoons olive oil
	Salt and freshly ground black pepper, to taste
1	medium red onion, thinly sliced
½	cup apple cider vinegar
8	slices Italian bread or 4 country rolls, split in half
½	cup mayonnaise
¼	cup prepared horseradish
2	cups arugula, lightly packed

RUB the steak with ¼ cup oil and season with salt and pepper. Rub salt and pepper in very well. Put the steak into a sealed bag or plastic container and let it rest in the refrigerator for at least 1 and up to 24 hours. The longer the meat marinates, the deeper the flavor of the final dish.

Preheat a grill pan over medium-high heat. Grill the meat on each side until it is cooked to preferred doneness. Check internal temperature with a thermometer. For rare, the temperature should be 125°F.; for medium, the thermometer should register 145°F.; and for well-done, the steak should be cooked to 160°F. Remove from heat and let the meat rest for 10 minutes.

Slice meat against the grain at a 45-degree angle. If you cut the meat with the grain or at no angle, the meat will be stringy and tough.

In a medium sauté pan, heat 1 tablespoon oil until it shimmers. Cook the onion with salt and pepper in the hot oil for 5 to 7 minutes on medium heat. Add vinegar, bring to a boil, and turn off heat. Let pickle for 10 minutes. Strain and cool.

Brush the bread with remaining tablespoon oil and grill until golden brown.

To make the aioli, combine the mayonnaise, horseradish, and salt and pepper, and mix well. Evenly spread the aioli on 4 slices of bread, top with steak, then onion, then the arugula. Top with other slices of bread and serve.

Grilled Chicken with Apple-Wood Smoked Bacon, Baby Swiss, and Blackberry Mayonnaise

Baby Swiss is a younger Swiss cheese that has a shorter aging process. The result is a delicate, mild flavor. Fresh blackberries are best for this dish, but frozen blackberries, or even blackberry jam, can be substituted. To spice it up a little, add some horseradish to the mayonnaise.

SERVES 2

2	boneless, skinless chicken breasts
1	tablespoon extra-virgin olive oil
	Salt and freshly ground black pepper, to taste
6	slices apple-wood smoked bacon
¼	cup fresh blackberries
¼	cup mayonnaise
4	slices Country White Bread (page 48)
2	slices baby Swiss

PREHEAT a grill pan for 10 minutes over high heat. Rub the chicken breasts with the oil and season with salt and pepper. Grill chicken for 3 to 4 minutes on each side until cooked through.

In a medium sauté pan, cook the bacon on medium heat for 5 to 7 minutes, or until crispy. Drain on a paper towel to absorb any excess grease.

Mix the blackberries and mayonnaise together thoroughly. Brush oil on the inside of the bread slices and grill until golden brown, about 5 minutes per side. Evenly spread the mayonnaise over the inside of the bread. Place the chicken on two bread slices. Place the bacon on top of the chicken breast and top with the cheese and the remaining slices of bread. Place on the grill for 1 minute to melt the cheese. Since the cheese is on top of the bacon and chicken, it will help to hold the sandwich together as it melts.

Asiago Roast Beef Sandwich

SERVES 1

2	tablespoons Horseradish Sauce (recipe follows)
2	slices Three-Cheese Bread (page 54)
1	leaf romaine lettuce
3–4	slices vine-ripened tomato, ¼ inch thick
3–4	slices red onion, ¼ inch thick
4	ounces roast beef, sliced wafer-thin
2	slices smoked Cheddar cheese

TO MAKE THE SANDWICH, spread the Horseradish Sauce over one side of one bread slice to cover end to end. On top of the sauce, layer the lettuce, tomato, onion, roast beef, and cheese. Top with the second slice of bread and serve.

Horseradish Sauce

MAKES 2 CUPS

½	cup prepared horseradish
1	cup sour cream
⅓	cup mayonnaise
1	tablespoon lemon juice
2	garlic cloves, minced
	Salt and freshly ground black pepper, to taste
1	tablespoon Dijon or whole-grain mustard

MIX all ingredients in medium bowl with wire whisk. Refrigerate for at least 30 minutes to allow the flavors to blend.

Broiled Shrimp and Tomato Banh Mi with Lime Mayonnaise and Avocado

Banh mi is a popular Vietnamese version of a New Orleans po' boy sandwich. It typically combines cooked meats or seafood, fresh vegetables, and a spicy sauce and is served warm on a toasted baguette or other crusty bread. Use a vegetable peeler to make the daikon and carrot shavings.

SERVES 4–6

1	pound raw shrimp (26 to 30 count or smaller), peeled and deveined (tails removed)
4	Roma tomatoes, sliced about ½ inch thick

MARINADE

¼	cup extra-virgin olive oil
2	tablespoons soy sauce
1	tablespoon fresh lime juice
1	tablespoon fresh ginger, peeled, minced
1	large garlic clove, minced
1	bird chile, thinly sliced
½	stalk lemongrass, peeled and finely minced
	Salt and freshly ground black pepper, to taste

LIME MAYONNAISE

4	large egg yolks
	Zest and juice of 1 small lime
1	small garlic clove, minced
1	tablespoon Dijon mustard
1½	cups extra-virgin olive oil
2	large baguettes or 4 demi-baguettes, sliced lengthwise and buttered
2	ripe avocados, peeled and cut into eighths
	Fresh cilantro sprigs
2	ounces daikon shavings
1	medium carrot, peeled and shaved

TOSS the shrimp and tomatoes together in a large bowl.

TO MAKE THE MARINADE, whisk together oil, soy sauce, lime juice, ginger, garlic, chile, and lemongrass. Season with salt and pepper. Toss with the shrimp and tomatoes. Marinate for at least 30 minutes and up to 2 hours.

TO MAKE THE MAYONNAISE, whisk the egg yolks with the lime zest, juice, garlic, and mustard in a double boiler while adding oil in a slow steady stream until thick and smooth. Season the mixture with salt and pepper. Remove from heat and cool.

Discard the marinade and broil the shrimp and tomatoes for about 1 to 2 minutes per side, or until the shrimp curls and turns pink.

If you are using whole baguettes, slice them into thirds. If using demis, slice them in half. Toast the baguettes and spread them liberally with mayonnaise. Fill the baguettes with the shrimp, tomatoes, avocado, cilantro, and daikon and carrot shavings.

Nicoise Salad on Baguette with Herb Roasted Fingerling Potatoes

SERVES 4–6

2	tablespoons red wine vinegar
1	tablespoon Dijon mustard
1	teaspoon honey
	Salt and freshly ground black pepper, to taste
½	cup + 2 tablespoons extra-virgin olive oil
½	pound fingerling potatoes, scrubbed and halved
2	tablespoons fresh herbs, chopped (any combination of thyme, rosemary, oregano, marjoram, basil, and parsley)
1	small garlic clove, minced
½	pound good-quality albacore tuna packed in olive oil (usually Spanish, French, or Italian in origin)
3	cups mixed greens, loosely packed
¼	cup kalamata olives, pitted
2	Roma tomatoes, thinly sliced
2	large hard-boiled eggs, sliced
¼	pound haricots verts (thin French green beans), blanched 1 minute in boiling, salted water, then cooled
2	large baguettes or 4 demi-baguettes, sliced lengthwise and buttered

PREHEAT oven to 450°F. In a medium bowl, whisk together the vinegar, mustard, honey, and salt and pepper. Drizzle ½ cup oil into the mixture while continuously whisking, until a smooth dressing is achieved. Set aside.

In a large bowl, toss the potatoes with the herbs, remaining 2 tablespoons oil, and garlic. Season with salt and pepper. Place on a baking sheet or in a shallow baking dish. Roast 30 to 40 minutes, or until golden and crisp.

Meanwhile, toss the tuna, greens, olives, tomatoes, eggs, and haricots verts with dressing to taste.

Reduce oven to 400°F. If you are using whole baguettes, slice them into thirds. If using demis, slice them in half. Toast the baguettes on baking sheets in the oven until golden brown, about 5 minutes per side. Stuff the toasted baguettes with the salad, and serve with the warm potatoes.

Goat Cheese, Tomato, and Thai Basil Panini

Panini are grilled Italian sandwiches typically made with white bread. The filling of the sandwich ranges from sweet to savory, from fruit and chocolate to meat and cheese. The crust often is brushed with olive oil before the sandwich is lightly grilled. A grill press such as the George Foreman grill is the best way to cook these sandwiches.

SERVES 2

1	tablespoon salted butter
4	slices Country White Bread (page 48) or brioche
3	tablespoons goat cheese
10	Thai basil leaves
1	large Roma tomato, cored, cut into 8 slices widthwise
	Salt and freshly ground black pepper, to taste

SPREAD butter on one side of each slice of bread and flip slices over so ingredients can be placed on the inside. Evenly spread goat cheese over the unbuttered sides of bread and distribute basil leaves and tomato on 2 slices. Sprinkle with salt and pepper. Top with a second slice of bread and grill in a press until golden brown, about 1 to 2 minutes per side. Cut the sandwiches in half and serve immediately.

Fontina and Fuji Apple Panini

Fontina is also known as Fontina Val d'Aosta after the Italian valley from which it comes. Semifirm yet creamy, Fontina is a cow's milk cheese with about 45 percent milk fat. Fontina has a mild, nutty flavor and a dark golden brown rind with a pale yellow interior dotted with tiny holes. Gruyère or mild Swiss also will work well in this recipe.

SERVES 2

1	tablespoon unsalted butter
4	slices Country White Bread (page 48) or brioche
4	ounces Fontina cheese, sliced
½	Fuji apple, cored, thinly sliced
	Salt and freshly ground black pepper, to taste

SPREAD the butter on one side of each bread slice and flip over. Distribute cheese evenly over the unbuttered sides of the bread slices. Arrange the apples on 2 bread slices, sprinkle with salt and pepper, and top with a second slice of bread. The cheese on both sides helps hold the sandwich together. Grill the sandwich in a press until golden brown and the cheese is melted, about 5 minutes.

Hazelnut Butter and Pluot Jam Panini

Pluots are a hybrid cross between a plum and an apricot. The flesh is very similar to that of a plum—sweet and delicious. If the peels bother you, cut an X in the bottom side of the fruit and blanch it in boiling water for 20 to 30 seconds. Then you will be able to peel the fruit easily. If you can't find pluots locally, plums or apricots can be substituted.

SERVES 2

1	tablespoon unsalted butter
4	slices Country White Bread (page 48)
1	cup toasted hazelnuts
⅛	teaspoon salt
1	tablespoon vegetable oil
¼	cup Pluot Jam (recipe follows)

SPREAD butter on one side of each bread slice. Puree hazelnuts in food processor with salt and oil until the consistency is like natural peanut butter.

Spread hazelnut butter on the unbuttered sides of 2 bread slices. Spread Pluot Jam on the unbuttered sides of the remaining 2 slices of bread and top with other slices of bread. Grill the sandwiches in a press until golden brown, about 2 to 4 minutes.

Pluot Jam

MAKES 2 CUPS

6	pluots, pitted and diced
1	cup sugar
	Juice of 1 orange
½	cup water
1	pinch salt
1	tablespoon dried fruit pectin

IN A THICK-BOTTOMED SAUCE POT, combine all ingredients. Cook over low heat for 20 to 30 minutes. The sauce will become very thick and pasty. Using a spatula, remove the sauce from the pot and puree in a food processor. Cool and store in an airtight container.

Pancetta, Pear, and Buffalo Mozzarella Panini

Buffalo mozzarella got its name from originally being made only from the milk of water buffalo. Today, it is most commonly made from a combination of water buffalo's and cow's milk. It almost always is packaged in whey or water. If you can't find pancetta, you can substitute high-quality bacon for this panini.

SERVES 2

1	tablespoon unsalted butter
4	slices Sourdough Bread (page 74)
4	slices pancetta
4	ounces buffalo mozzarella, thinly sliced
½	pear, cored, thinly sliced
	Salt and freshly ground black pepper, to taste

SPREAD butter evenly on one side of each bread slice. Preheat a sauté pan over medium-high heat and cook pancetta. Evenly distribute the cheese on the unbuttered sides of all 4 slices of bread; then on 2 slices, layer the pear and pancetta, and season with salt and pepper. Top with a second slice of bread. Grill the sandwiches in a press until golden brown and the cheese is melted, about 5 minutes.

Poblano-Pulled Pork with Avocado and Cilantro Crema on Country White

SERVES 10

	Zest and juice of 2 oranges
	Zest and juice of 2 limes
	Zest and juice of 1 grapefruit
1	teaspoon ground cumin
1	large head garlic, minced
2	large poblano chiles, seeded and minced
3	sprigs fresh thyme, stemmed and coarsely chopped
½	cup extra-virgin olive oil
	Salt and freshly ground black pepper, to taste
3–4	pounds pork butt, whole
4	ripe avocados, peeled and diced
2	cups Mexican *crema* or sour cream
1	bunch fresh cilantro, coarsely chopped, plus 5 sprigs for assembly
2	loaves Country White Bread (page 48), sliced and buttered

PREHEAT oven to 325°F. To make the marinade, combine the zests and juices, cumin, garlic, poblanos, and thyme in the bowl of a food processor, adding the olive oil in a slow stream. Season with salt and pepper.

In a large roasting pan, rub three-quarters of the marinade all over the pork and into any cavities. Season with plenty of salt and pepper. Roast for at least 4 to 6 hours, basting with the marinade at least once every hour. Allow the pork to rest at least 30 minutes and then shred the meat by pulling it apart with your fingers or two forks while still warm. When all of the pork has been pulled, toss with remaining marinade.

Blend 3 of the avocados in a food processor with the *crema* and cilantro. Then fold in the remaining diced avocado and season with salt and pepper.

Preheat oven or grill to 400°F. Toast the bread on baking sheets in the oven, or grill, until golden brown, about 5 minutes per side. Assemble by spreading the *crema* mixture on the unbuttered sides of the bread, and filling with the pulled pork and remaining cilantro.

INTERNATIONAL BREAD BITE: MEXICO

The corn tortilla is the staple bread of Mexico, crossing all socio-economic and geographic lines. Many view the tortilla as a simple food, but the finely-tuned process of crafting the perfect tortilla using traditional methods can take up to four hours. Two ingredients, corn and water, and three tools are necessary: a *metate*, or volcanic flat stone, a *mano*, or cylindrical roller, and a concave clay plate known as a *comal*. For preparation, the corn is boiled for several hours in lime-infused water and then rinsed with clean water. The kernels are then ground between the *metate* and *mano* to produce a dough. This dough is then formed into small balls and flattened out with the hands to form a flat cake. To finish the process, the cake is placed on the *comal* and flipped one time for a completed tortilla.

The work is difficult and long, but the reward is the incredible tortilla: an essential piece of many traditional Mexican dishes such as tacos, quesadillas, gorditas, chalupitas, and chilaquiles.

Southern Fried Chicken on Ciabatta with Bread-and-Butter Pickles and Garlic Mayonnaise

The leg of the chicken is best to use for this because of the skin, which will add to the tenderness and flavor of the dish. A breast also will work but should be pounded thin before cooking. To pound a chicken breast, place it between two layers of plastic wrap; then using either a meat mallet or a rolling pin, lightly pound the meat to desired thinness.

SERVES 2

2	loaves ciabatta, sliced lengthwise
4	whole garlic cloves
1	tablespoon olive oil
2	chicken legs, deboned
	Salt and freshly ground black pepper, to taste
1	cup all-purpose flour
1	cup peanut oil
¼	cup mayonnaise
6	slices bread-and-butter pickle

PREHEAT oven to broil. With the inside of the bread facing the broiler, broil for 1 minute. Remove and decrease the oven temperature to 400°F.

Toss the garlic in olive oil and roast for 20 minutes, or until soft. After the garlic cools, place it on a cutting board. Using the side of a chef's knife, press the garlic back and forth to form a paste.

Lightly season both sides of the chicken legs with salt and pepper. Place the flour in a paper bag or dish and coat the chicken with the flour.

Heat the peanut oil in a cast-iron or heavy sauté pan to 350°F. Carefully place the chicken in the oil and fry for 2 minutes per side. Do not flip the chicken more than once or it will absorb oil and become greasy. Place the fully cooked chicken on a paper towel to absorb excess oil.

In a small bowl, whisk together the roasted garlic, mayonnaise, and salt and pepper. Spread the mayonnaise on 2 pieces of the toasted bread and top with chicken, then the pickles, and the other pieces of bread.

Virginia Ham and Gruyère with Honey Dijon Mayonnaise on Sourdough

Using honey-baked ham adds a nice flavor, but either omit the honey in the sauce or reduce the amount used to achieve the desired taste.

SERVES 2

1	tablespoon mayonnaise
1	tablespoon Dijon mustard
1	tablespoon honey
1	pinch salt
1	tablespoon butter
4	slices Sourdough Bread (page 74)
4	ounces Gruyère cheese, thinly sliced or grated
½	pound baked Virginia ham, sliced

IN A SMALL BOWL, mix the mayonnaise, mustard, honey, and salt. Spread the butter on the outside of the bread. Spread the mayonnaise mixture on the inside of the bread. Evenly distribute the cheese on the inside of all 4 slices of bread and top with ham. Put two slices together, ham sides in. In medium sauté pan, cook the sandwiches on medium-low heat until the cheese melts and the bread is golden brown.

Soups, Salads & Sides

When used in soups, salads, and sides, bread is most versatile. In its simplest form, artisan bread is diced for croutons and stuffing and hollowed for bread bowls. Used creatively, artisan loaves thicken stews and soups and blend smoothly with eggs and spices to form tender dumplings. In the recipes that follow, you will see how rustic loaves create new flavors in the most unlikely dishes.

[soups]

Five-Onion Soup with Scallion and Gruyère Croutons

SERVES 6–8

3	large yellow onions, halved and sliced (pole to pole)
3	red onions, halved and sliced
6	shallots, halved and sliced
3	leeks (white parts only), halved lengthwise and sliced crosswise
3	cups scallions (greens reserved for croutons), sliced
1	large garlic clove, minced
	Salt and freshly ground black pepper, to taste
¼	cup extra-virgin olive oil
1	750-ml bottle red wine
1	small bunch thyme (12 sprigs), cut into 4-inch lengths
6	quarts Beef Stock (recipe follows)
1	baguette, sliced into ½-inch coins
1	cup Gruyère cheese, grated

IN A 12-QUART STOCKPOT, sauté the onions, shallots, leeks, scallion whites, garlic, and a heavy pinch of salt in 2 tablespoons oil until the onions begin to caramelize. Deglaze with the red wine. Add the thyme and stock to the pot. Bring the soup to a boil, reduce heat to low, and simmer for at least 1 hour. Adjust the seasoning with salt and pepper.

While the soup is simmering, preheat the oven to broil. Toss the bread coins with remaining 2 tablespoons oil and place flat on a sheet pan. Toss the scallion greens with the Gruyère, and top each coin with the mixture. Bake on a rack in the middle of the oven for 3 minutes and then transfer to the broiler to lightly brown the tops. The cheese should be bubbly. Ladle the soup into bowls and top with croutons.

Beef Stock

MAKES 6 QUARTS

5   pounds beef bones
6   ounces tomato paste
2   medium onions, coarsely chopped
3   medium carrots, peeled and chopped into 1-inch pieces
3   ribs celery, chopped into 1-inch pieces
2   gallons cold water

PREHEAT oven to 350°F. Roast bones in a roasting pan in the oven for 30 minutes. Remove from oven and spread the tomato paste all over the bones. Return to oven and roast for an additional 30 minutes.

Place onions, carrots, and celery in a large stockpot, and add the beef bones and any roasting liquids. Add the water and bring to a boil. Turn down to simmer and cook for 3 hours, skimming the fat during the cooking process with a ladle. Strain through a chinoise or cheesecloth.

Corn and Oyster Mushroom Chowder with Ciabatta Crackers

The finished chowder has a special sweetness that comes from "milking" the corn cobs. Holding the top of each cob, slice downward to remove all of the kernels. Then run the back of the knife (the dull side) over the cobs to extract the sweet juices and add to the chowder with the corn. Yellow or white corn will work equally well in this dish.

SERVES 8

1	cup cold whole milk
2	large egg whites
16	slices ciabatta, ¼ inch thick
	Salt and freshly ground black pepper, to taste
3	tablespoons unsalted butter
1	large onion, cut into 1-inch dice
4	ribs celery, cut into ¼-inch slices
1	large garlic clove, minced
4	large sprigs fresh thyme, stemmed and coarsely chopped
1	pound oyster mushrooms, torn into quarters from top to stem
1	pound Russet potatoes, scrubbed and sliced into ¼-inch pieces
4	ears of corn, kernels cut off cob, scraped for juice, and cobs reserved
¼	cup dry white wine
2	quarts hot Vegetable Stock (recipe follows) or Chicken Stock (page 184)
2	cups heavy cream

PREHEAT oven to 400°F. To make crackers, whisk the milk and egg whites until frothy and dip each bread slice quickly into the batter. Place on a baking sheet in the oven and bake until golden brown, 10 to 15 minutes. Sprinkle with salt immediately upon removing from oven and set aside to cool.

In a heavy-bottomed dutch oven or stockpot, melt the butter over medium heat. Sauté the onion, celery, garlic, thyme, and mushrooms. Add the potatoes, corn kernels, and juices scraped from the cobs. Cook an additional minute; then add the wine, stock, and reserved cobs. Bring to a boil, and reduce to simmer for approximately 15 minutes, or until the potatoes are fork tender. Remove the corn cobs, add the cream, and season with salt and pepper. Remove from heat, and allow to rest for 5 to 10 minutes. Serve with ciabatta crackers.

Vegetable Stock

MAKES 6 QUARTS

2	gallons cold water
3	medium onions, coarsely chopped
3	medium carrots, peeled and chopped into 1-inch pieces
3	ribs celery, chopped into 1-inch pieces
1	leek, halved lengthwise, rinsed, and chopped into 1-inch pieces
1	bunch fresh parsley
1	bunch fresh thyme
10	black peppercorns
3	tomatoes
5	garlic cloves, smashed

COMBINE all ingredients in large stockpot. Bring to a boil, reduce to a simmer, and cook for 3 hours. Strain through a chinoise or cheesecloth.

Ribollita with Black-Eyed Peas, Kale, and Gremolata

Ribollita *is a twice-cooked Italian soup traditionally made with* cavolo nero, *a black Tuscan cabbage, and cannellini beans. Here the black-eyed peas and kale make a nice substitute. To make an equally hearty vegetarian version, substitute 1 ounce smoked tofu—found at specialty stores—for the bacon, and a vegetable stock or water for the chicken stock. Gremolata is a traditional Italian mixture of parsley, garlic, and citrus used to flavor meats and soups. The bread in this recipe serves as both a flavor enhancer and a thickening agent, showing its versatility.*

SERVES 6

½	cup extra-virgin olive oil, plus extra for garnish
1	medium yellow onion, diced
1	large carrot, peeled and sliced
1	rib celery, cut crosswise into ¼-inch pieces
1	large garlic clove, thinly sliced
2	slices bacon, cooked and diced
2	large sprigs fresh thyme, stemmed and coarsely chopped
1	head kale, torn into bite-size pieces
4	quarts Chicken Stock (recipe follows)
1	pound black-eyed peas, cooked, or 1 16-ounce can
	Salt and freshly ground black pepper, to taste
12	slices Country White Bread (page 48), roughly torn
¼	cup fresh Italian parsley leaves, packed
	Zest of 4 small lemons
1	whole large garlic clove

IN A 6-QUART STOCKPOT, heat the oil over medium heat. Sweat the onion, carrot, celery, sliced garlic, bacon, and thyme in the oil until the vegetables begin to wilt. Add the kale and stock and bring to a boil. Add the black-eyed peas and reduce the heat. Simmer for 25 minutes, tasting and seasoning occasionally with salt and pepper. Stir in the bread and remove from heat. Allow to cool completely (this portion of the dish can be made a day ahead).

To make the *gremolata,* finely chop the parsley, lemon zest, and garlic together on a cutting board.

When you are ready to serve, bring the soup to a boil, adding hot water or more stock if it appears too thick. Taste, adjusting seasoning as necessary, and serve with a generous pinch of the *gremolata* and a drizzle of olive oil.

Chicken Stock

MAKES 6 QUARTS

1	fresh bay leaf or 4 dried
1	bunch fresh thyme
½	bunch fresh tarragon stems
1	bunch fresh parsley
15	black peppercorns
1	4-pound chicken, cut into parts
2	medium onions, coarsely chopped
2	medium carrots, peeled and chopped into 1-inch pieces
2	ribs celery, chopped into 1-inch pieces
2	gallons cold water

MAKE a bouquet garni by wrapping the bay leaf, thyme, tarragon, parsley, and peppercorns inside a piece of cheesecloth and tying with kitchen twine.

Rinse the chicken well, drain, and pat dry. Coarsely chop with a meat cleaver.

Place onions, carrots, celery, and bouquet garni in a large stockpot; then top with the chicken parts. Add the water. Bring to a boil, turn down to a simmer, and cook for 3 hours. Do not boil the stock, or it will be cloudy and somewhat creamy. Skim the fat off the top during the cooking process with a ladle. Strain through a chinoise or cheesecloth.

Cream of Artichoke Soup with Chervil and Fried Artichokes

SERVES 8

4	quarts water
8	whole artichokes
	Juice of 1 lemon
2	tablespoons olive oil
8	tablespoons (1 stick) unsalted butter
7	cups Vegetable Stock (page 183) or Chicken Stock (page 185)
6	slices Country White Bread (page 48), crusts removed
1	cup fresh chervil, packed
	Vegetable oil, for frying
1	cup heavy cream
	Salt and ground white pepper, to taste

BRING the water to a boil in an 8-quart pot.

Trim the top third off each artichoke and discard, along with the stems. The bottom two-thirds of each artichoke should remain in tact. Set 2 artichoke bottoms aside. Quarter the other 6 artichoke bottoms and toss with the lemon juice and olive oil. Transfer quartered artichokes, lemon juice, and oil to the water and boil for 10 minutes. Drain artichokes.

Melt 4 tablespoons of butter in a 4-quart pot and add the cooked artichokes. Stir them over low heat for about 10 minutes. Be careful not to let the butter burn. Pour in the stock and boil for 20 minutes.

Melt the remaining 4 tablespoons of butter. Dip the bread slices into the melted butter and sauté over medium heat until golden brown, 3 to 4 minutes per side. Add the cooked bread to the pot with the artichokes and simmer for 5 minutes. Remove from heat and add the cream. Season with salt and pepper to taste.

Puree the soup in a food processor, then run it through a food mill until smooth. Cool 1½ cups of soup in the freezer. Puree the chervil in the chilled soup. Make sure the soup is cold before you puree the chervil, because if it is hot, the chervil will turn brown. Heat the chervil mixture to 200°F.

Thinly slice the reserved artichoke bottoms and fry in vegetable oil until golden brown, about 2 to 3 minutes. Drain on a paper towel to absorb excess oil.

Evenly distribute the hot soup among 8 bowls. Drizzle the chervil mixture over the soup, and garnish with the fried artichokes.

Chicken and Dumplings

SERVES 6

1   large onion, cut into 1-inch dice

4   ribs celery, cut into ¼-inch slices

4   medium carrots, peeled and cut into ¼-inch slices

1   large whole garlic clove, peeled

4   large sprigs fresh thyme

2   tablespoons extra-virgin olive oil

3   quarts water

    Salt and freshly ground black pepper, to taste

1   large (about 5 pounds) chicken, quartered, or 5 pounds chicken legs and thighs

1   loaf Country White Bread (page 48), crusts removed and cut into ½-inch cubes

3   cups cold water

3   large eggs, beaten

    Paprika, to taste

IN A LARGE STOCKPOT or dutch oven over medium heat, sweat the onion, celery, carrots, garlic, and thyme in the oil for 7 to 10 minutes. Add the 3 quarts of water and season with salt and pepper. Add the chicken, bring to a simmer, and continue simmering 25 to 35 minutes, or until the chicken is cooked through. Remove chicken from the pot while the broth continues to simmer and pull all of the meat off the bones. Return the meat to the pot while preparing the dumplings.

Soak the bread in the cold water for 1 minute. Squeeze as much water out of the bread as possible. In a medium bowl, work the eggs, paprika, and salt and pepper into the bread to form a dough.

Skim the fat off of the top of the broth with a spoon. Add the dumpling dough, one spoonful at a time, into the simmering soup. Cook 2 to 3 minutes, or until the dumplings float. Adjust seasoning and serve.

Country Bread and Tomato Soup with Mashed Basil Oil

SERVES 8

½ cup fresh basil leaves, packed
¾ cup extra-virgin olive oil
  Salt and freshly ground black pepper, to taste
3 large garlic cloves, thinly sliced
1 teaspoon crushed red pepper flakes
1 teaspoon dried oregano
2 28-ounce cans whole, peeled tomatoes (organic plum or San Marzano) or 12 ripe Roma tomatoes, peeled
1 quart water or Vegetable Stock (page 183)
¼ cup dry red wine
1 loaf Country White Bread (page 48), torn into bite-size pieces

WITH A MORTAR AND PESTLE, mash the basil well with ½ cup of the oil and season with salt and pepper. If you do not have a mortar and pestle, this step can be done in a food processor. To preserve the rustic taste and appearance of this infused oil, take care to pulse the ingredients very gently. Set the mashed basil oil aside.

In an 8-quart stockpot, heat the remaining ¼ cup oil over medium-low heat. Cook the garlic, pepper flakes, and oregano just until the garlic begins to sizzle. Crush the tomatoes with your hands over the stockpot, including all juices that come from the tomatoes. Add the water or stock and red wine and bring to a boil. Reduce heat and simmer for 10 to 15 minutes. Taste for seasoning and adjust as needed. Stir in the bread and remove from the heat. Serve immediately, drizzling the hot soup liberally with the mashed basil oil.

Roasted Garlic Soup with Country White Bread

SERVES 8

¾	cup extra-virgin olive oil
16	garlic cloves, peeled
4	4-inch sprigs fresh oregano, stemmed, or 1 teaspoon dried oregano
1	loaf Country White Bread (page 48), torn into bite-size pieces
2	quarts Vegetable Stock (page 183) or Chicken Stock (page 185)
1	tablespoon hot Spanish or Hungarian paprika
	Salt and freshly ground black pepper, to taste

IN A MEDIUM SAUCEPAN over medium heat, simmer the oil with the garlic and oregano until the garlic is light golden brown, 5 to 10 minutes. Make certain not to allow the oil to get too hot, or the garlic will brown too quickly and be chewy. Strain and reserve the infused oil, and transfer garlic and oregano to a small bowl.

In a 4-quart stockpot, fry the bread in ½ cup infused oil, until golden, about 2 to 3 minutes. Remove and place in serving bowls.

Return the garlic, oregano, and remaining oil to the stockpot and add the stock. Bring to a boil and add the paprika. Season with salt and pepper. Puree the soup in a food processor until smooth. Pour the hot soup over the bread and serve immediately.

Mussel and Tomato Stew
with Bird Chile Mollica

Common in Italian cooking, a mollica *is a Sicilian-style bread crumb mixture. Because it's so easy to make—as simple as toasting good-quality bread crumbs with olive oil and seasonings—a* mollica *is a superior alternative to store-bought bread crumbs. In this dish, it adds spice and thickens the texture of the stew.*

SERVES 6

½	cup + 2 tablespoons extra-virgin olive oil
2	cups white bread crumbs
3	bird chiles, minced
	Salt and freshly ground black pepper, to taste
2	large shallots, minced
2	large garlic cloves, minced
4	pounds mussels, debearded and rinsed well
½	cup dry red wine
1	28-ounce can whole, peeled tomatoes (organic plum or San Marzano) or 6 ripe Roma tomatoes, peeled
2	cups water
½	cup fresh basil leaves, torn and packed

TO MAKE THE MOLLICA, heat ½ cup oil in a sauté pan over medium-high heat. Pan fry the bread crumbs with the chiles until golden brown. Season with salt and pepper and set aside.

In an 8-quart pot over medium-high heat, sauté the shallots and garlic in remaining 2 tablespoons oil, and then add the mussels. Deglaze with the red wine. Hand-crush the tomatoes into the pot and add the water. Bring to a boil and simmer until the mussels open (discard any that do not open). Stir in the basil and remove from heat. Ladle into bowls and serve with a generous spoonful of the *mollica*.

salads

Asian Sesame Chicken Salad

SERVES 1

2   wonton wrappers
    Canola oil, for frying
2   tablespoons sliced almonds
4   cups romaine lettuce, torn into bite-size pieces, loosely packed
1   tablespoon fresh cilantro, chopped
3   ounces boneless, skinless chicken breast, grilled and sliced thinly
    on a bias
¼   cup Panera Bread Asian Sesame Dressing (recipe follows)
1   tablespoon sesame seeds

PREHEAT the oven to 350°F. To prepare wonton strips, cut wonton wrappers into ¼-inch strips. In a deep skillet, pour canola oil to a depth of 2 to 3 inches. Heat oil to 365°F. Carefully drop wonton slices into hot oil and fry for about 30 seconds, or until crisp and golden. Remove with slotted spoon and drain on paper towels.

Arrange almonds in a single layer on a sheet pan. Toast in the oven for 5 minutes, toss nuts, then toast for an additional 5 minutes, or until golden. Remove from pan to cool.

To make the salad, toss the lettuce, cilantro, wonton strips, chicken, and dressing in a large mixing bowl until combined. Place the mixture on a serving plate. Sprinkle with sesame seeds and almonds and serve.

Panera Bread Asian Sesame Dressing

¼ cup rice wine vinegar
¼ cup toasted sesame oil
2 tablespoons soy sauce
1 teaspoon toasted sesame seeds
1 teaspoon crushed red pepper flakes
¾ cup canola or vegetable oil

COMBINE all ingredients except canola oil in a medium mixing bowl with a wire whisk. Once ingredients are combined, slowly pour in the oil while whisking to form an emulsion.

Roasted Beet Caprese with Buffalo Mozzarella and Three-Seed Croutons

SERVES 4

2	large beets (preferably a mix of purple and golden), greens removed
¼	cup + 2 tablespoons olive oil
	Salt and freshly ground black pepper, to taste
¾	cup water
1	loaf three-seed bread, such as Panera Bread Three-Seed, cut into ½-inch cubes
8	ounces buffalo mozzarella, cut into ½-inch cubes
¼	cup fresh basil, chiffonade
1	cup arugula leaves
1	tablespoon balsamic vinegar

PREHEAT oven to 400°F. Wash beets to remove any dirt. In medium roasting pan, toss the beets with 2 tablespoons oil and season with salt and pepper. Pour the water in the bottom of the pan, cover, and bake for 30 to 40 minutes depending on beet size. To check doneness, stick a toothpick into the center of beets; if they are soft in the center, the beets are cooked. Leave the oven at 400°F. Cool, remove the skins by hand, and cut the beets in half; then cut each half into 4 slices.

Toss the bread cubes in 2 tablespoons oil and season with salt and pepper. Place on a baking sheet in the oven. Bake for 8 minutes, toss lightly, and bake for an additional 7 minutes until a crust forms but the bread is still soft in the center. Toss the toasted bread with the cheese, basil, remaining olive oil, and salt and pepper.

To serve, layer 4 beet slices in a semicircle on each salad plate. Beside the beets make a small pile of arugula and top with the bread-and-cheese mixture. Drizzle with balsamic vinegar and serve.

Warm Salad of Blackened Tuna, Ciabatta, Watercress, and Champagne Vinaigrette

SERVES 4

2	tablespoons champagne vinegar
1	teaspoon sugar
	Salt and freshly ground black pepper, to taste
¼	cup + 2 tablespoons extra-virgin olive oil
3	cups ciabatta bread, cut into 1-inch cubes
1	teaspoon garlic powder
2	tablespoons peanut or canola oil
8	ounces tuna steaks, albacore or yellowfin
2	tablespoons blackening seasoning
1	cup watercress

PREHEAT oven to 400°F. To make the champagne vinaigrette, whisk the vinegar, sugar, and salt and pepper to taste in a mixing bowl or combine in a blender. Slowly drizzle in ¼ cup olive oil, whisking fast to emulsify.

Toss bread in remaining 2 tablespoons olive oil, garlic powder, and salt and pepper. Evenly layer the bread cubes on a baking sheet and bake in the oven for 10 to 15 minutes, rotating sheet 180 degrees halfway through. The cubes should not be crisp throughout, just toasted long enough to form a nice crust; the inside should remain somewhat chewy.

Heat the peanut oil in a medium heavy-bottomed skillet. Coat the entire tuna with the blackening seasoning. Sear the fish for 20 to 30 seconds per side for a rare center or a bit longer for a more well-done fish. Remove the tuna from the pan and let it rest for 5 minutes. Then cut against the grain into thin slices.

Lightly combine the bread, tuna, watercress, and vinaigrette to coat all ingredients. Serve warm.

Salad of Ciabatta, Celeriac, Grapes, Walnuts, and Apple

SERVES 4

2	cups ciabatta bread, cut into ½-inch cubes
2	tablespoons olive oil
1	cup celeriac (celery root), thinly sliced
½	cup seedless grapes, halved
½	cup walnuts, toasted, slightly crushed
1	apple, cored, quartered, and thinly sliced
½	cup mayonnaise
2	tablespoons fresh chives, chopped into ½-inch pieces
	Salt and freshly ground black pepper, to taste

PREHEAT oven to 400°F. Toss the ciabatta in 1 tablespoon of the olive oil. Place the bread cubes in a single layer and toast them in the oven on a baking sheet until golden brown, about 10 minutes. Remove from oven and let cool to room temperature. After bread is cooled, place it into a large bowl. Toss together with celeriac, grapes, walnuts, apple, mayonnaise, chives, and remaining oil. Season with salt and pepper.

 MENU
FAVORITE

Greek Salad

SERVES 1

4	cups romaine lettuce, torn into bite-size pieces, loosely packed
10	slices red onion rings, ¼ inch thick
1	medium vine-ripened tomato, cut into 6 wedges
5	kalamata olives, pitted
¼	cup Panera Bread Greek Salad Dressing (recipe follows)
2	tablespoons feta cheese, crumbled
2	pepperoncini, 3 inches long
	Freshly ground black pepper, to taste

IN A LARGE MIXING BOWL, toss the lettuce, onion, tomato, olives, and dressing until combined. Place the mixture on a serving plate. Top with feta, pepperoncini, and black pepper and serve.

Panera Bread Greek Salad Dressing

MAKES 2 CUPS

½	cup red wine vinegar
2	teaspoons garlic, minced
2	teaspoons shallot, minced
2	teaspoons fresh oregano, finely chopped
2	teaspoons fresh basil, chiffonade
1	tablespoon Dijon or whole-grain mustard
	Salt and freshly ground black pepper, to taste
1½	cups extra-virgin olive oil

COMBINE all ingredients except oil in a medium mixing bowl with a wire whisk. Once ingredients are combined, slowly pour in the olive oil while whisking to form an emulsion.

Eggless Caesar Salad with Olive Croutons

SERVES 6

1	loaf Kalamata Olive Bread (page 52), sliced ¼ inch thick and cut into ½-inch strips
1¼	cups extra-virgin olive oil
½	teaspoon fresh thyme, chopped
	Salt and freshly ground black pepper, to taste
1	tablespoon red wine vinegar
1	tablespoon fresh lemon juice
1	tablespoon Dijon mustard
1	teaspoon Worcestershire sauce
1	teaspoon Tabasco sauce
1	large garlic clove, minced
1	large head romaine lettuce, rinsed and torn into bite-size pieces
½	cup Parmigiano-Reggiano cheese, grated

PREHEAT oven to 400°F. To make the croutons, toss the bread strips, ½ cup oil, thyme, and salt and pepper in a medium bowl. Place on a baking sheet in the oven and toast just until golden brown, 8 to 10 minutes.

In a medium bowl, whisk the vinegar, lemon juice, mustard, Worcestershire sauce, Tabasco sauce, and garlic until combined. Continue whisking, adding remaining ¾ cup oil in a slow, steady stream. Season well with salt and pepper. The dressing should have a consistency similar to mayonnaise.

To serve, toss the lettuce with the dressing, croutons, and half of the cheese in a large salad bowl. Top the salad with the remaining cheese.

Panzanella with Heirloom Tomatoes and Roasted Garlic

This traditional Italian bread salad is perfect for summer days and picnics.

SERVES 4

1	head garlic
¾	cup olive oil
1	loaf Kalamata Olive Bread (page 52) or ciabatta, sliced ½ inch thick
1	tablespoon fresh thyme leaves, chopped
	Salt and freshly ground black pepper, to taste
2	large heirloom tomatoes, cored and cut into ½-inch dice
¼	cup balsamic vinegar
½	cup fresh basil leaves, chiffonade

PREHEAT oven to 350°F. Cut the top off of the garlic head and roast for 25 minutes, or until soft. Squeeze the roasted garlic into a small bowl and mix with oil. Use a butter knife to spread the garlic-flavored oil onto each slice of bread. Set the remaining garlic oil aside. Cut the bread slices into ½-inch cubes and toss with the thyme and salt and pepper.

Arrange bread cubes evenly on a baking sheet in the oven and bake for 20 minutes, rotating the pan 180 degrees after 10 minutes. Remove from the oven and let the croutons cool on the baking sheet.

Meanwhile, toss the tomatoes with the remaining garlic oil, the vinegar, and basil. Season with salt and pepper. Let the tomatoes marinate while the bread is toasting. Toss the bread with the tomato mixture and serve immediately.

INTERNATIONAL BREAD BITE: MIDDLE EAST

Bread is regarded so highly in the Middle East that in some Arabic dialects, it is often referred to as *esh,* meaning "life." In many regions, people historically were nomads; traveling was their way of life. Bread was adapted to serve as both a food and a utensil for delivering food. Traditional flatbread could be baked quickly in makeshift ovens fueled with wood, corn cobs, or even camel dung, and it continues to be a staple in the daily diets of Middle Eastern cultures.

Even though this bread is flat, with few exceptions, the bread is not unleavened. The ancient Egyptians mastered the art of leavening bread and by the twelfth century BC were producing more than forty varieties of bread. These Middle Eastern breads are primarily made with wheat, as history states the first wheat to be cultivated came from this region thousands of years ago.

Perhaps the most recognizable Middle Eastern bread is the pita. Made from wheat flour, yeast, water, and a little salt, this pocket bread can be quickly prepared and quickly baked. During a brief, but hot, baking period, a pocket is formed, which can be stuffed with meats, cheeses, and vegetables. Some say the pita was the first "fast food" in the world.

Focaccia Fattoush with Preserved Lemon Vinaigrette

Fattoush is a traditional Middle Eastern bread salad typically made with pita bread. Any other flatbread would work equally well. Z'atar is a Middle Eastern spice blend made with sumac, lemon peel, and dried herbs. Z'atar and preserved lemons can be found at gourmet stores or Middle Eastern specialty shops.

SERVES 8–10

2	preserved lemons, rind only, minced
¼	cup fresh lemon juice
1	teaspoon honey
1	cup extra-virgin olive oil
	Salt and freshly ground black pepper, to taste
1	loaf Focaccia Bread (page 53), cut into ½-inch cubes
4	Roma tomatoes, cut into ¼-inch slices
¼	cup fresh mint, chopped, packed
¼	cup fresh parsley, chopped, packed
¼	cup fresh basil, chopped, packed
½	cup kalamata olives, pitted
1	European seedless cucumber, thinly sliced
1	poblano chile, roasted, seeded, and diced
1	tablespoon *z'atar*

WHISK the lemon rinds, juice, and honey in a medium bowl, while adding the oil in a slow, steady stream until thoroughly incorporated. Add salt and pepper to taste.

In a large, non-reactive bowl, toss the bread, tomatoes, herbs, olives, cucumber, poblano, and *z'atar* with the dressing. Taste and add salt and pepper if desired.

Fandango Salad

SERVES 1

2	tablespoons walnuts, chopped
3	cups field greens, loosely packed
1	cup romaine lettuce, torn into bite-size pieces, loosely packed
¼	cup Panera Bread Raspberry Vinaigrette (recipe follows)
2	tablespoons Gorgonzola cheese, crumbled
8-10	slices Mandarin orange

PREHEAT the oven to 350°F. Arrange the walnuts in a single layer on a sheet pan. Toast for 5 minutes, toss nuts, then toast for an additional 5 minutes, or until golden. Remove from pan to cool.

In a medium mixing bowl, toss field greens, romaine, and vinaigrette until well combined. Place the mixture on a serving plate. Top with the cheese, walnuts, and orange slices and serve.

Panera Bread Raspberry Vinaigrette

MAKES 1 CUP

¼	cup raspberry vinegar
2	teaspoons Dijon mustard
2	tablespoons raspberry jam
2	teaspoons shallot, minced
	Salt and freshly ground black pepper, to taste
¾	cup extra-virgin olive oil

COMBINE all ingredients except oil in a medium mixing bowl with a wire whisk. Once ingredients are combined, slowly pour in the olive oil while whisking to form an emulsion.

Arugula Salad with Lemon Dressing and Baked Goat Cheese

SERVES 4

	Zest and juice of 2 lemons
¼	cup olive oil
	Salt and freshly ground black pepper, to taste
4	cups arugula
1	4-ounce log herbed goat cheese, sliced into 4 equal portions
½	cup white bread crumbs

PREHEAT oven to 400°F. In a large mixing bowl, combine lemon zest and juice. Slowly drizzle in the oil while whisking to emulsify. Season the dressing with salt and pepper, to taste. Toss the arugula with the dressing.

Generously coat the goat cheese rounds with the bread crumbs. Transfer to a baking sheet and bake until the bread crumbs are a light golden brown and the cheese is heated through, 3 to 4 minutes.

Divide the arugula among 4 plates and top each serving with a goat cheese round.

[sides]

Turkey Sausage and Sage Stuffing

Most stuffings are made with dried breads or croutons that break down in the oven to form a traditional base. The following stuffing recipes rely on herbs and spices, nuts, and stock to provide the bulk of flavor and texture. Using cubed artisan bread as the foundation adds a unique twist to this favorite side dish, building on the strong characteristics of the bread itself. Experiment by substituting various artisan breads or bread crumbs and see how these subtle changes can add new life to your own favorite family recipes.

Pork, chicken, or any other type of sausage will work well in this stuffing recipe. Just remember that the leaner the meat, the less fat, so a little more oil might be needed to sauté the vegetables. Cornbread or challah also are delicious breads to use for this dish.

SERVES 10–12

12	cups Italian bread, cut into 1-inch cubes
1¾	cups Chicken Stock (page 185)
1	cup half-and-half
2	large eggs, lightly beaten
12	ounces turkey sausage, broken into 1-inch pieces
3	medium onions, diced
3	ribs celery, diced
2	tablespoons (¼ stick) unsalted butter
2	tablespoons fresh thyme leaves, chopped
¼	cup fresh sage leaves, chopped
3	garlic cloves, minced
	Salt and freshly ground black pepper, to taste

PREHEAT oven to 250°F. Evenly layer bread pieces on baking sheets in the oven. Dry the bread in the oven for 40 to 50 minutes, rotating the sheets 180 degrees halfway through cooking. After drying, place bread in large mixing bowl.

Increase oven temperature to 400°F. In a large mixing bowl, whisk together the stock, half-and-half, and eggs. Add the bread and toss lightly to coat. Set aside.

Heat a heavy-bottomed skillet over medium-high heat. Add turkey sausage and cook, stirring occasionally, until sausage is no longer pink, about 5 to 7 minutes. With a slotted spoon, remove the sausage from the pan and drain on a paper towel. Transfer sausage to a bowl.

Add about half of the onions and celery to the fat in skillet, stirring occasionally, until soft and translucent, about 5 minutes. Transfer the onion mixture to the bowl with the sausage. Return the skillet to the heat, add the butter, and cook remaining onions and celery until soft, about 5 minutes. Stir in the thyme, sage, and garlic. Cook until fragrant, 30 to 45 seconds, and season with salt and pepper. Add this mixture and the sausage mixture to the bread and mix gently (try not to break up the bread too much).

Spray a 12 × 16-inch baking dish or pan with non-stick cooking spray, or grease with butter, and evenly spread the stuffing in the dish. Cook the stuffing for 30 to 35 minutes, or until golden brown. Let the stuffing rest for 5 minutes before serving.

Creole Oyster Stuffing

To save time and mess at home, ask your fishmonger or seafood market to shuck the oysters and save the liquid from the shells for you.

SERVES 8

4	tablespoons (½ stick) unsalted butter
1	small sweet onion, diced
4	ribs celery, diced
1	green bell pepper, seeded and diced
1	garlic clove, minced
4	scallions (white and green parts), sliced
3	cups (15–20 large or 20–30 medium) shucked oysters, liquid reserved
6	cups white or sourdough bread crumbs
1	cup Chicken Stock (page 185)
1	tablespoon Tabasco sauce
2	tablespoons Creole seasoning or 1 teaspoon each of ground cayenne pepper, dried oregano, dried basil, paprika, and garlic powder, combined
	Salt and freshly ground black pepper, to taste

PREHEAT oven to 400°F. In a medium sauté pan over medium heat, melt the butter and sauté the onion, celery, bell pepper, garlic, and scallions for 1 to 2 minutes, or until the onion is translucent. Fold in the oysters, bread crumbs, stock, Tabasco sauce, and seasonings and transfer to a buttered 9 × 13-inch baking dish. Bake for 20 to 25 minutes, or until golden brown on top.

Wild Mushroom Stuffing

You can replace the stock with the rehydrating liquid, or heat the stock and use it to rehydrate the mushrooms. Just be sure to strain the rehydrating liquid before adding it to the stuffing, to remove the sediment from the mushrooms.

SERVES 10–12

1¾	cups Chicken Stock (page 185)
¼	pound dried mushrooms (chanterelles, morels, black trumpets, porcini, or a mixed blend)
12	cups Italian bread, cut into 1-inch cubes
1	cup half-and-half
2	large eggs, lightly beaten
2	tablespoons extra-virgin olive oil
3	medium onions, diced
3	ribs celery, diced
	Salt and freshly ground black pepper, to taste
2	tablespoons (¼ stick) unsalted butter
¾	pound fresh mushrooms (shiitake, crimini, chanterelles, morels, porcini, or any combination)
3	garlic cloves, minced
2	tablespoons fresh thyme leaves, minced
2	tablespoons fresh summer savory, minced

PREHEAT oven to 250°F. Heat the stock in a medium saucepan just until hot. Place the dried mushrooms in a small bowl and cover with the hot stock. Let the mushrooms rehydrate for 25 minutes and drain, reserving the liquid.

Evenly layer the bread cubes on baking sheets. Dry the bread in the oven for 40 to 50 minutes, rotating the sheets 180 degrees halfway through cooking. After drying, place bread in large mixing bowl.

Increase oven temperature to 450°F. Strain the reserved mushroom liquid to remove any sediment. In a large mixing bowl, whisk together the liquid, half-and-half, and eggs. Add bread and toss lightly to coat. Set aside.

In large heavy-bottomed sauté pan or skillet, heat the oil over medium heat. Sauté the onions and celery with salt and pepper until soft, about 5 minutes, and remove. Add butter to the pan and sauté the fresh mushrooms with salt and pepper until most of the liquid has cooked out, about 5 to 7 minutes.

Add the rehydrated mushrooms and cook for 2 to 3 minutes. Add the garlic and herbs, season with salt and pepper, and cook for about 1 more minute. Combine the mushrooms and onion mixtures with the bread mixture and stir gently to combine (try not to break the bread into smaller pieces).

Spray a 12 × 16-inch baking dish or pan with non-stick cooking spray, or grease, with butter, and evenly spread the stuffing in the pan. Cook the stuffing for 30 to 35 minutes, or until golden brown. Let the stuffing rest for 5 minutes before serving.

Potato-Fennel Gratin

A gratin is any dish topped with cheese or bread crumbs mixed with butter, and heated under the broiler until brown and crispy. Try substituting different types of bread crumbs, such as wheat or pumpernickel, to uncover new flavors.

SERVES 10–12

3	fennel bulbs, cored and cut into ⅛-inch slices, leaves reserved
½	cup + 2 tablespoons extra-virgin olive oil
	Salt and freshly ground black pepper, to taste
1½	cups whole milk
1½	cups heavy cream
3	pounds Yukon Gold potatoes, cut into ⅛-inch slices
4	cups white bread crumbs
8	tablespoons (1 stick) salted butter

PREHEAT oven to 350°F. In a baking dish, toss the fennel slices in 2 table-spoons olive oil and season with salt and pepper to taste. Roast for 20 minutes. Leave oven at 350°F.

Combine the milk and cream in a large saucepan and season with salt and pepper. Cook over medium heat until the liquid reaches 190–200°F. Blanch the potatoes in the hot liquid for 5 to 7 minutes. The starch will be released from the potatoes as they cook, thickening the milk and cream. Remove the potatoes from the pan and reserve the milk-cream mixture.

Coarsely chop the fennel leaves and mix with the bread crumbs and remaining ½ cup oil. Season with salt and pepper. Spread the bread crumbs evenly on a baking sheet in the oven and toast for 10 minutes, stirring halfway through.

Coat the bottom and sides of a 9 × 13-inch baking dish with butter. Evenly layer the potatoes on the bottom, overlapping as you go. Then evenly layer fennel, then thin slices of butter, then a thin layer of bread crumbs. Repeat the process, reserving ¾ cup of the bread crumbs. Before putting this final layer of bread crumbs on top, pour the milk–cream mixture over the gratin. Heavily top with the final layer of bread crumbs. It is very important to pour the cream over the gratin before you place the final layer of bread crumbs, or you will not get a brown, crunchy top.

Bake for 45 minutes to 1 hour, uncovered, then broil for 3 to 5 minutes to brown the top. Allow gratin to rest 10 minutes before serving.

Summer Squash Gratin

SERVES 10–12

5	pounds summer squash (crookneck, zucchini, pattypan), sliced lengthwise into ⅛-inch pieces
3	leeks (white parts only), sliced lengthwise with layers separated, and rinsed under cold water
1	cup extra-virgin olive oil
	Salt and freshly ground black pepper, to taste
1	cup whole milk
2	cups heavy cream
¼	cup fresh thyme leaves, packed
4	cups white bread crumbs
4	tablespoons (½ stick) salted butter

PREHEAT oven to 400°F. In a baking dish, toss the squash and leeks in ½ cup oil. Season with salt and pepper. Roast for 15 to 20 minutes and cool.

Decrease oven temperature to 350°F. In a medium saucepan over medium heat, combine the milk, cream, and half the thyme. Season with salt and pepper. Bring to a boil and continue cooking for 15 minutes, or until the liquid reduces to about 2 cups. Remove from heat and set aside.

Mix the bread crumbs with remaining ½ cup oil. Mix in the remaining thyme and season with salt and pepper. Spread the bread crumbs evenly on a baking sheet and toast for 10 minutes in the oven, stirring halfway through.

Generously butter the sides of a 9 × 13-inch baking dish. Line with parchment paper and lightly butter the top of the paper. Start layering the squash and leeks, then the bread crumbs, then small pats of butter. Repeat the process, reserving ¾ cup bread crumbs. Season the top with salt and pepper. Pour the cream over the top and finish with the remaining bread crumbs. It is very important to pour the cream over the gratin before you place the final layer of bread crumbs, or you will not get a brown, crunchy top.

Bake, uncovered, for 1 hour, rotating halfway through, and then broil for 3 to 5 minutes to brown the top. Allow the gratin to rest for 10 minutes before serving.

Four-Cheese Gemelli

SERVES 6–8

5	cups gemelli pasta
4	tablespoons (½ stick) unsalted butter
¼	cup all-purpose flour
2	cups whole milk
½	cup Gruyére cheese, grated
½	cup white Cheddar cheese, grated
¼	cup Stilton cheese, crumbled
1	cup white bread crumbs
½	cup freshly grated Parmigiano-Reggiano cheese
	Salt and freshly ground black pepper, to taste

PREHEAT oven to 350°F. Cook the pasta according to the package directions. Drain and transfer the pasta to a buttered 9 × 13-inch baking dish.

In a sauté pan, melt the butter over medium heat. Mix in the flour with a whisk and cook and stir for 5 to 7 minutes over medium heat to form a roux and cook out the flour flavor.

In a medium saucepan, heat the milk over medium heat and slowly whisk into the roux. This will form one of the six mother sauces, a béchamel. Slowly mix in the Gruyère, Cheddar, and Stilton cheeses. After the sauce has thickened and the cheese has completely melted, pour over the cooked pasta in the baking dish. Spread everything into an even layer. Top with the bread crumbs and the Parmigiano-Reggiano cheese.

Place the dish on the bottom rack of the oven and bake for 1 hour, rotating the dish 180 degrees after 30 minutes. Broil for 3 to 5 minutes to brown the top. Let cool for 10 minutes before serving.

Eggplant, Tomato, and Grana Padana

Slowly aged, Grana Padana is a delicate but flavorful cow's milk cheese from Italy. If you can't find it at your local market, you can substitute Parmigiano-Reggiano for this dish.

SERVES 10–12

2	large eggplants, sliced into ½-inch rounds
½	cup extra-virgin olive oil
	Salt and freshly ground black pepper, to taste
4	large beefsteak tomatoes, sliced ½ inch thick
3	cups white bread crumbs, seasoned with salt and pepper
1	cup Grana Padana, shaved or grated

PREHEAT oven to 400°F. In a baking dish, toss eggplant rounds in ¼ cup oil. Season with salt and pepper. Roast for 20 minutes or until soft. (You also can grill the eggplant slices for a nice, smoky flavor.)

In another baking dish, toss the tomato rounds in ¼ cup oil. Season with salt and pepper, and roast for 7 to 10 minutes.

Decrease oven temperature to 350°F. Butter the sides and bottom of a 9 × 13-inch baking dish or coat with a non-stick spray. Layer half of the eggplant slices; then top with half of the tomato slices, half of the bread crumbs, and half of the cheese. Repeat this order with the remaining half of each ingredient. Bake for 15 minutes.

Desserts

Bread pudding, fondue, and tiramisu are just a few of the countless desserts that highlight bread. Artisan breads smoothly transition from savory to sweet, blending effortlessly with marmalades, berries, port wine, and chocolates. Fruit-laden crostini and bread-crumbed brown Bettys are worthy rewards at the end of a meal that celebrates the range of artisan breads.

Bing Cherry Cheesecake with Chocolate Crust

Using whole-wheat bread crumbs for the crust will produce a more rich and complex flavor in the final dessert.

SERVES 12

CRUST

2	cups whole-wheat bread crumbs
¼	cup sugar
¼	cup light brown sugar
8	tablespoons (1 stick) unsalted butter, melted
½	cup semisweet chocolate chips
½	teaspoon salt

FILLING

1½	pounds cream cheese, softened
1	cup sugar
1	tablespoon vanilla extract
	Zest of 1 lemon
4	large eggs
1	cup heavy cream
2	cups Bing cherries, pitted and halved

PREHEAT oven to 500°F. To make the crust, combine the bread crumbs, sugars, butter, chocolate chips, and salt in a medium bowl until the bread crumbs are thoroughly coated. Press the mixture into the bottom of a 9-inch springform pan.

FOR THE FILLING, cream the cheese, sugar, vanilla extract, and lemon zest together. Beat in the eggs, one at a time, then the cream, and blend until smooth (if the batter is still lumpy, you can press it through a sieve). Fold in the cherries. Pour the batter into the prepared pan, place in the oven, and immediately reduce the heat to 325°F.

Bake for 45 minutes to 1 hour, or until the filling is set. Cool thoroughly at room temperature before chilling. This cake freezes well for up to 3 months.

New York Style Cheesecake with Cinnamon Raisin Crust

SERVES 12

CRUST

2	cups cinnamon raisin bread crumbs
¼	cup sugar
¼	cup light brown sugar
8	tablespoons (1 stick) unsalted butter, melted
½	teaspoon salt

FILLING

1½	pounds cream cheese, softened
1	cup sugar
1	tablespoon vanilla extract
	Zest of 1 lemon
4	large eggs
1	cup heavy cream

PREHEAT oven to 500°F. To make the crust, combine the bread crumbs, sugars, butter, and salt in a medium bowl until the bread crumbs are thoroughly coated. Press the mixture into the bottom of a 9-inch spring-form pan.

FOR THE FILLING, cream the cheese, sugar, vanilla extract, and lemon zest together. Beat in the eggs, one at a time, then the cream, and blend until smooth (if the batter is still lumpy, you can press it through a sieve). Pour the batter into the prepared pan, place in the oven, and immediately reduce the heat to 325°F.

Bake for 45 minutes to 1 hour, or until the filling is set. To test for doneness, gently shake the pan. The filling should be firm. Cool thoroughly at room temperature before chilling. This cake freezes well for up to 3 months.

Pumpkin Cheesecake
with Whole-Wheat Crust

SERVES 12

CRUST

2 cups whole-wheat bread crumbs
¼ cup sugar
¼ cup light brown sugar
8 tablespoons (1 stick) unsalted butter, melted
½ teaspoon salt

FILLING

1½ pounds cream cheese, softened
1½ cups cooked, mashed pumpkin
1 cup sugar
1 tablespoon vanilla extract
1 teaspoon ground cinnamon
1 teaspoon ground nutmeg
1 teaspoon ground ginger
  Zest of 1 lemon
4 large eggs
1 cup heavy cream

PREHEAT oven to 500°F. To make the crust, combine the bread crumbs, sugars, butter, and salt in a medium bowl until the bread crumbs are thoroughly coated. Press the mixture into the bottom of a 9-inch spring-form pan.

FOR THE FILLING, cream the cheese, pumpkin, sugar, vanilla extract, spices, and lemon zest together. Beat in the eggs, one at a time, then the cream, and blend until smooth (if the batter is still lumpy, you can press it through a sieve). Pour the batter into the prepared pan, place in the oven, and immediately reduce the heat to 325°F.

Bake for 45 minutes to 1 hour, or until the filling is set. Cool thoroughly at room temperature before chilling. This cake freezes well for up to 3 months.

Pineapple Fritters with Lavender

Traditional fritters are a deep-fried batter often containing bite-size pieces of meats, fruits, or vegetables. A favorite dish at carnivals and other community celebrations, fritters are easy to make, providing a tasty treat any time of the day. Bread crumb fritters are similar to their battered brethren, but offer additional flavors to complement or contrast with the ingredient inside. Artisan bread crumbs also contribute a light and crumbly texture—a recognizable contrast to the traditional variety.

SERVES 8

    Canola oil, for frying
2   cups white or sourdough bread crumbs
2   tablespoons sugar
1   tablespoon lavender buds
2   large eggs, beaten
½   cup whole milk
1   small ripe pineapple, peeled, cored, and cut into finger-size sticks
    Powdered sugar, for dusting

IN A DEEP, HEAVY-BOTTOMED SKILLET, pour the oil to cover a 2-inch depth. Heat the oil to 350°F. over medium-high heat.

Combine the bread crumbs, sugar, and lavender in a small bowl and set aside. In a separate bowl, whisk together the eggs and milk.

Roll the pineapple fingers, one at a time, first in the egg mixture, then the bread crumb mixture. Fry the pineapple in the oil for 3 to 4 minutes, until golden brown, flipping halfway through. Serve warm with the powdered sugar.

Papaya Fritters with
Melted Vanilla Bean Ice Cream

SERVES 8

> Canola oil, for frying
> 1 cup vanilla bean ice cream, melted at room temperature just to the consistency of a very heavy sauce
> 2 ripe papayas, peeled, seeded, and cut into eighths
> 2 cups white or sourdough bread crumbs
> Powdered sugar, for dusting

IN A DEEP, HEAVY-BOTTOMED SKILLET, pour canola oil to cover a 2-inch depth. Heat the oil to 350°F. over medium-high heat. Set ½ cup of the melted ice cream aside.

Roll the papaya fingers, one at a time, in ½ cup of the ice cream and then the bread crumbs. Fry the papaya in the oil for 3 to 4 minutes, until golden brown, flipping halfway through. Serve warm with the powdered sugar and reserved melted ice cream.

Mango Fritters with Coconut

SERVES 8

	Canola oil, for frying
2	cups white or sourdough bread crumbs
2	tablespoons sugar
1	cup coconut, shredded
2	large eggs, beaten
½	cup unsweetened coconut milk
4	ripe mangoes, peeled, seeded, and cut into finger-size sticks
	Powdered sugar, for dusting

IN A DEEP, HEAVY-BOTTOMED SKILLET, pour canola oil to cover a 2-inch depth. Heat the oil to 350°F. over medium-high heat.

Combine the bread crumbs, sugar, and coconut in a small bowl and set aside. In a separate bowl, whisk together the eggs and coconut milk.

Roll the mango fingers, one at a time, first in the egg mixture, then in the bread crumb mixture. Fry the mango in the oil for 3 to 4 minutes, until golden brown, flipping halfway through. Serve warm with the powdered sugar.

Banana Fritters with Rum

Manzanos are a smaller, sweeter version of bananas. Just 3 to 5 inches long, they ripen to a complete black color, when they have their best flavor. They are drier than regular bananas and have delicate undertones of papaya and apple. If you can't find them in your local market, you can substitute 8 regular bananas, cut in half, for these fritters.

SERVES 8

	Canola oil, for frying
2	cups white or sourdough bread crumbs
2	tablespoons sugar
1	teaspoon ground cinnamon
2	large eggs, beaten
¼	cup whole milk
2	tablespoons dark rum
16	Manzano bananas
	Powdered sugar, for dusting

IN A DEEP, HEAVY-BOTTOMED SKILLET, pour canola oil to cover a 2-inch depth. Heat the oil to 350°F. over medium-high heat.

Combine the bread crumbs, sugar, and cinnamon in a small bowl and set aside. In a separate bowl, whisk together the eggs, milk, and rum.

Roll the bananas, one at a time, first in the egg mixture, then the bread crumb mixture. Fry the bananas in the oil for 3 to 4 minutes, until golden brown, flipping halfway through. Serve warm with the powdered sugar.

Apple Fritters with Hard Cider

SERVES 8

          Canola oil, for frying
2   cups white or sourdough bread crumbs
2   tablespoons sugar
1   teaspoon ground cinnamon
2   large eggs, beaten
½   cup hard apple cider
4   small Granny Smith apples, peeled, cored, and quartered
     Powdered sugar, for dusting

IN A DEEP, HEAVY-BOTTOMED SKILLET, pour canola oil to cover a 2-inch depth. Heat the oil to 350°F. over medium-high heat.

Combine the bread crumbs, sugar, and cinnamon in a small bowl and set aside. In a separate bowl, whisk together the eggs and cider.

Roll the apple pieces, one at a time, first in the egg mixture, then the bread crumb mixture. Fry the apples in the oil for 3 to 4 minutes, until golden brown, flipping halfway through. Serve warm with the powdered sugar.

Blueberry Buttermilk Bread Pudding with Maple Syrup

Bread pudding is a centuries-old dessert originally created from leftover or day-old breads and a simple mix of milk and spices. Once considered the poor man's pudding, this popular dessert has come a long way from its humble roots. Incorporating a splendid variety of unique flavor combinations, today's bread puddings start with a custard base and add spirits, fruits, syrups, and teas to bring new depths of sophistication and character to a once meager loaf. The availability and variety of artisan breads continue to bring new tastes and textures to this beloved dessert.

Bursting with flavors from blueberries, buttermilk, and maple syrup, this pudding also makes a terrific entree for a weekend or holiday brunch.

SERVES 8

8	large eggs
1	quart buttermilk
1	cup sugar
1	tablespoon vanilla extract
2	cups fresh or thawed frozen blueberries
8	cups Country White Bread (page 48) or Sourdough Bread (page 74), cut into ½-inch cubes
1	cup pure maple syrup, warmed
	Powdered sugar, for dusting

PREHEAT oven to 375°F. Butter a 9 × 13-inch baking dish.

In a large bowl, whisk together the eggs, buttermilk, sugar, and vanilla extract. Fold in the blueberries and bread. Transfer to the prepared dish and cover tightly with aluminum foil.

Bake 30 minutes, uncover, and then bake an additional 10 minutes. Serve with the maple syrup and powdered sugar.

Milk Chocolate Bread Pudding
with Oolong Tea Sauce

SERVES 8

8	large eggs
1	cup sugar
1	quart half-and-half
1	tablespoon vanilla extract
8	ounces milk chocolate chunks
8	cups ½-inch Sourdough Challah Bread (page 76) cubes

OOLONG TEA SAUCE

2	cups half-and-half
2	tablespoons oolong tea leaves
4	large egg yolks
½	cup sugar

Powdered sugar, for dusting

PREHEAT oven to 375°F. Butter a large loaf pan or 9 × 13-inch baking dish.

In a large bowl, whisk together eggs, sugar, half-and-half, and vanilla extract. Fold in chocolate and bread and transfer to prepared pan or dish. Cover tightly with aluminum foil. Bake for 30 minutes, uncover, and then bake an additional 10 minutes.

TO MAKE THE SAUCE, bring the half-and-half to a boil in a small saucepan and then remove from heat immediately. Add the tea leaves and steep for 5 to 7 minutes. Pour the infused half-and-half through a fine mesh strainer to remove the leaves.

In a medium bowl, whisk together the egg yolks and sugar. Temper the yolk mixture by slowly adding the infused half-and-half, ½ cup at a time, then immediately whisk it into the mixture, making certain not to scramble the eggs by working too quickly.

Transfer the mixture to a double boiler over medium-high heat, and stir to thicken, 6 to 8 minutes, or until it coats the back of a spoon. Serve with the warm pudding and powdered sugar.

Individual Raisin Pecan Bread Puddings with Orange Marmalade

SERVES 6

2	cups heavy cream
1	pinch salt
1	vanilla bean, split and scraped
¾	cup sugar
3	large egg yolks
1	boule Raisin Pecan White Bread (page 51), crusts removed and cut into ½-inch cubes
1	tablespoon unsalted butter
6	tablespoons orange marmalade
	Powdered sugar, for dusting

PREHEAT oven to 350°F. In a saucepan, heat the cream, salt, vanilla bean, and ½ cup sugar over medium heat. Bring to a simmer; stir to dissolve sugar and make sure the mixture doesn't scorch. Remove from the heat.

In a large bowl, beat the egg yolks for 1 to 2 minutes until thick and frothy. Temper the egg yolks by very gradually pouring in the hot cream mixture and whisking constantly, until all is incorporated and evenly blended. Be careful not to scramble the eggs by working too quickly.

Add the bread cubes to the custard mixture and mix well so that all the bread is submerged in the liquid. Let it soak for 15 minutes.

Butter the bottom and sides of 6 individual ramekins and coat with the remaining sugar. Fill each ramekin halfway with the bread pudding. Make an indentation in the center of each and fill with a tablespoon of orange marmalade. Cover with the remaining bread pudding, filling each to the top.

Place the ramekins on a baking sheet and bake for 25 minutes until set. Dust with powdered sugar before serving.

Butterscotch Bread Pudding with Bourbon and Pecans

SERVES 8

¾   cup light brown sugar

4   tablespoons (½ stick) unsalted butter

1   tablespoon vanilla extract

¼   cup bourbon whiskey

8   large eggs

½   cup sugar

1   quart half-and-half

2   cups pecan pieces

8   cups ½-inch Country White Bread (page 48) or Sourdough Bread (page 74) cubes

Powdered sugar, for dusting

PREHEAT oven to 375°F. Butter a 9 × 13-inch baking dish.

To make the butterscotch sauce, combine the brown sugar, butter, vanilla extract, and bourbon in a small saucepan over medium heat. Simmer the mixture, stirring until the sugar is dissolved and the mixture is smooth in consistency. Cool ½ cup and set aside.

In a large bowl, whisk together the eggs, sugar, half-and-half, and the cooled butterscotch sauce. Fold in pecans and bread, transfer to the prepared dish, and cover tightly with aluminum foil. Bake 30 minutes, uncover, and then bake an additional 10 minutes. Gently shake the pan to make sure the pudding has set.

Serve with remaining butterscotch sauce, warmed, and powdered sugar.

Summary Berry Pudding

SERVES 8

6   cups fresh berries (any mix of raspberries, blackberries, blueberries, or small strawberries)
2   cups sugar
1   tablespoon vanilla extract
2   tablespoons port, Vin Santo, or other dessert wine
12 slices Country White Bread (page 48), crusts removed and sliced ½ inch thick

IN A SMALL SAUCEPAN over medium heat, bring 3 cups berries, sugar, vanilla extract, and wine to a soft simmer for about 30 minutes, or until the berries begin breaking down. Remove from heat and fold in the remaining berries.

Using half of the bread, slightly overlapping, line an 8- or 9-inch glass or stainless steel serving bowl, or a trifle dish. Pour half of the berry sauce evenly over the bread. Then layer half of the remaining bread on top, add the remainder of the sauce, and top the dish with the remaining bread.

Weigh the pudding down by placing another similar-size bowl directly on top and placing a heavy object, such as a can, inside. Place the dish inside a larger pan to capture any berry juices that may escape. Allow the dish to chill for at least 6 hours, and up to 24 hours. Invert mold onto a serving platter.

Banana Charlotte with Butter Rum Sauce

In this sweet treat, the bread caramelizes as it cooks, producing a tartlike shell around the banana and butter rum filling.

SERVES 6–8

8	tablespoons (1 stick) unsalted butter, plus extra for the pan
1	cup light brown sugar, packed
¼	cup dark rum
1	tablespoon ground cinnamon
½	teaspoon salt
12	slices Country White Bread (page 48), crusts removed
6	large, ripe bananas (about 6 cups), sliced into ½-inch pieces
	Powdered sugar, for dusting
	Vanilla ice cream
1	quart vanilla bean ice cream

PREHEAT oven to 375°F. Butter an 8- or 9-inch brioche pan or ovenproof trifle mold to the top.

To make the butter rum sauce, melt the butter in a small saucepan over medium heat. Stir in the brown sugar, rum, cinnamon, and salt. Simmer the sauce just until the alcohol has cooked out of the rum (when the aroma is less like alcohol and more like caramel), about 5 minutes. Remove from heat.

Drizzle one quarter of the sauce in the prepared pan and tilt the edges to distribute evenly. Line the pan with 6 to 8 bread slices, so that they overlap slightly. Drizzle one quarter more of the sauce over the bread. Toss another one quarter of sauce with the sliced bananas, and pour half into the mold. Cover with 3 to 4 bread slices, pour the remaining bananas over them, cover with the remaining bread, and drizzle with the remaining sauce. Cover tightly with aluminum foil.

Bake 30 minutes, uncover, and then bake an additional 15 minutes. Invert the charlotte while still warm, dust with powdered sugar, and serve with ice cream.

Basic Bread Crumb Streusel

Streusel is a sweet, crumbly topping used on cakes, muffins, and pies. From the German word meaning "to sprinkle or scatter," streusel traditionally is made from a mixture of butter, flour, sugar, and spices. Substituting artisan bread crumbs for flour will result in a lighter, crispier texture. Using different varieties of bread, such as Raisin Pecan White Bread (page 51) or Honey Wheat (page 56), will add additional flavor to a streusel.

MAKES 1 QUART

2	cups white or sourdough bread crumbs
4	tablespoons (½ stick) unsalted butter
¼	cup sugar
¼	cup light brown sugar
1	teaspoon ground cinnamon
½	teaspoon salt
¼	cup walnuts or pecans (optional)

PULSE all ingredients in the bowl of a food processor until well combined. Store in an airtight container in the refrigerator for up to 2 weeks until ready to use.

INTERNATIONAL BREAD BITE: GERMANY

While there are more than four hundred varieties of German bread, the most popular bread product of this country is undoubtedly the pretzel. The first pretzel was created sometime between the fifth and seventh centuries by a group of monks. The pretzel that we enjoy today evolved from a baker's mistake. The baker put the formed dough in the oven without letting it rise and forgot about it. Baked too long and unrisen, the pretzels grew dark, hard, and crunchy—and turned out to be a great success among the people. The German word *brezel* is derived from the Latin *brachium,* meaning "arm"—as the bread baker's leftover strips of dough were folded and twisted to resemble a person's arms crossed in prayer. In a religious context, the pretzel came to stand for good fortune, prosperity, and spiritual wholeness.

The pretzel also became an integral part of German wedding ceremonies. The couple wished on and broke a pretzel similar to the sharing of a wishbone. Following the break, both husband and wife ate what remained as a symbol of their oneness.

Pear Brown Betty

You can substitute apples for the pears, if you prefer.

SERVES 6–8

4	Bosc or D'anjou pears, cored and sliced ¼ inch thick
1	tablespoon fresh lemon juice
1	tablespoon all-purpose flour
¼	cup sugar
1	tablespoon whiskey or vanilla extract
2	cups Basic Bread Crumb Streusel (page 234)
	Vanilla ice cream or whipped cream

PREHEAT oven to 400°F. In a medium bowl, toss the sliced pears with the lemon juice, flour, sugar, and whiskey or vanilla extract. Pour into a 9-inch deep-dish pie pan or large skillet (cast iron is great for this). Top evenly with the streusel, and bake 30 to 40 minutes, or until a golden crust forms and the filling is bubbly. Serve warm with ice cream or whipped cream.

Zinfandel-Poached Pears
with Raisin Pecan Streusel

SERVES 8

1	750-ml bottle zinfandel or other bold, dark red wine (not blush)
1½	cups sugar
	Zest and juice of 1 orange
1	sprig fresh thyme
8	small Bosc or D'anjou pears, peeled, cored, and halved
2	cups Basic Bread Crumb Streusel (page 234), made with Raisin Pecan White Bread (page 51)
	Vanilla ice cream or whipped cream

PREHEAT oven to 400°F. In a large saucepan, bring the wine, sugar, orange zest and juice, and thyme to a boil over high heat. Reduce the heat to medium. Add the pears, and poach, turning occasionally, about 20 minutes, or until medium tender to touch.

Top each pear with ¼ cup streusel and then place streusel-side up in a 9 × 13-inch baking dish. Bake 15 to 20 minutes, or until golden on top. Serve warm with ice cream or whipped cream.

Strawberry Rhubarb Crisp with Shiraz

Shiraz is the flagship grape variety in Australia, and the resulting wine has grown in popularity worldwide in recent years. Shiraz wine is a rich, spicy red, with delicate notes of plum and blackberry.

SERVES 6–8

2	pints ripe strawberries, hulled and quartered
4	large stalks rhubarb, trimmed and sliced into ¼-inch pieces
2	tablespoons all-purpose flour
¼	cup sugar
½	cup shiraz wine
2	tablespoons fresh lemon juice
2	cups Basic Bread Crumb Streusel (page 234)
	Vanilla ice cream

PREHEAT oven to 400°F. In a large bowl, toss the strawberries and rhubarb with the flour, sugar, wine, and lemon juice. Pour into a 9-inch deep-dish pie pan or large skillet (cast iron is great for this). Top evenly with streusel. Bake 30 to 40 minutes, or until a golden crust forms and the filling is bubbly. Serve warm with ice cream.

INTERNATIONAL BREAD BITE: AUSTRALIA

Australia's settlers came from all across the globe and brought with them a diversity of baking influences and formulas. Australia, while well versed in many styles of baking, does have one signature bread that its people claim as their own: the damper. This bread was designed to be made outdoors, in the wilds of the Australian bush. The dough, made from wheat flour and water and flavored with spices, is formed into cakes and baked on hot stones. The word *damper* comes from the fact that the fire was damped down so that the embers were just the right temperature for cooking the bread. Damper bread is also made by wrapping the dough around sticks and then placing it over the fire. After the bread is done, the baking sticks are removed and the holes filled with butter or cheese.

There is also a bit of irony when it comes to bread and the bread baking industry in Australia. In the 1700s, much of the country's population was made up of convicts who were deported from England. Many of these criminals were sent to this far-off land for stealing bread in their native land. The main diet of these first settlers consisted of flour, and many worked in mills or bakeries, forming the first organized system of farming and processing of wheat. From this early start, Australia has grown to become the fourth-largest wheat-producing country in the world, behind the United States, Canada, and the European Union.

Shoo-Fly Pie with Chai and Streusel Topping

SERVES 8

2	cups all-purpose flour
2	tablespoons sugar
2	teaspoons salt
10	tablespoons (1¼ sticks) unsalted butter, cubed and chilled
1	large egg yolk
3–4	tablespoons ice water
¾	cup molasses
2	large eggs, lightly beaten
2	teaspoons baking soda
1	cup strong-brewed, hot Chai tea
2	cups Basic Bread Crumb Streusel (page 234)

PREHEAT oven to 400°F. In a medium bowl, combine the flour, sugar, and salt. With a pastry blender, fork, or food processor, cut the cold butter into the dry ingredients until the mixture resembles coarse crumbs. Stir in the egg yolk and water to form a cohesive dough, making certain not to overmix as this will make the dough chewy as opposed to flaky.

Roll the dough out to a 9-inch round and then refrigerate it for at least 15 minutes. Line a 9-inch pie pan with the chilled crust, trimming the edges as necessary. Bake the crust, covered with parchment and weighted with rice or beans, for 10 to 15 minutes, or until somewhat dry to the touch.

Reduce heat to 325°F. To make the filling, whisk together molasses, eggs, and baking soda and then slowly add the Chai tea. Pour the filling into the crust, top with the streusel, and bake for 35 to 45 minutes, or until the filling is set. Serve warm or at room temperature.

White and Dark Chocolate Fondue
with Torn Challah

If you don't own a double boiler, the chocolate can be melted in separate glass bowls placed over small saucepans of boiling water on the stove. To avoid burning the chocolate while melting, make sure each bowl is suspended over the boiling water but not in direct contact with it.

SERVES 8

1   pound white chocolate, chopped

1   pound semisweet or bittersweet chocolate, chopped

2   cups heavy cream

2   tablespoons Kahlúa, Baileys, Frangelico, or Kirsch (optional)

2   pinches salt

1   loaf Sourdough Challah Bread (page 76), torn into bite-size pieces and warmed

Strawberries or other fresh fruit for dipping

IN A SMALL SAUCEPAN, bring cream to a boil and then immediately remove from heat. Melt dark and white chocolate halfway in separate double boilers. Pour 1 cup of hot cream over each and add a pinch of salt and 1 tablespoon liqueur to each. Transfer the chocolate-cream mixtures to separate fondue pots, stirring as needed. Using skewers, dip pieces of bread and fruit into fondue and serve.

Cinnamon French Toast Ice-Cream Sandwiches

SERVES 4

5	large eggs, beaten
½	teaspoon ground cinnamon
½	teaspoon vanilla extract
2	tablespoons (¼ stick) unsalted butter
8	slices Cinnamon Raisin White Bread (page 50), ½ inch thick and crusts removed
½	gallon ice cream of choice, such as vanilla, rum raisin or butter pecan, softened

IN A SMALL BOWL, mix eggs, cinnamon, and vanilla extract.

Melt butter in a skillet over medium-high heat. Dip sliced bread into egg mixture and grill in the skillet, about 45 seconds per side. Allow bread to cool on a rack.

Spread a scoop of ice cream onto a piece of bread and top with a second piece of bread to make a sandwich. Wrap sandwich with waxed paper or plastic wrap and place in freezer for at least 1 hour.

Lemon-Lime Granita with Honey Challah Toast

SERVES 6

¾	cup sugar
¾	cup water
¾	cup fresh lemon juice
¾	cup fresh lime juice
6	slices challah
1–2	tablespoons honey
1–2	tablespoons extra-virgin olive oil

IN A SMALL SAUCEPAN, bring the sugar and water to a boil. Cool and whisk in the juices. Transfer to a small mixing bowl and place in the freezer. Whisk the granita every 2 hours until slushy.

Preheat broiler. Place the bread slices on a baking sheet and drizzle with honey and olive oil. Broil until bubbly, about 1 minute. Serve toasted bread slices with the finished granita.

Pear Pecan Crostini

SERVES 10–12

10	ounces blue cheese (Roquefort, Gorgonzola, or Stilton)
5	tablespoons heavy cream
15	slices Cinnamon Raisin White Bread (page 50), crusts removed and cut into 1½-inch squares
2	Bartlett pears, peeled, cored, and thinly sliced into wedges about 1½ inches long
⅓	cup pecan halves, thinly sliced crosswise

PREHEAT oven to 350°F. In a small bowl, combine the cheese and cream with a fork or wooden spoon until mixture is soft enough to spread but not runny. Set aside.

Spread bread squares on baking sheets. Toast in the oven until lightly golden, about 6 minutes on each side. Remove from oven. Spread 1 heaping teaspoon cheese mixture on each crostini. Top each with a pear wedge and garnish with pecan slices. Serve at room temperature.

Tiramisu with Challah and Port

SERVES 6

4	large egg yolks
½	cup sugar
¼	cup + 2 tablespoons port wine
1	teaspoon vanilla extract
½	cup heavy cream
1	cup mascarpone cheese
¾	cup espresso
1	loaf challah, crusts removed and cut into 3 × ½-inch fingers
¼	cup cocoa powder
	Shaved bittersweet chocolate

IN A DOUBLE BOILER OVER MEDIUM HEAT, whisk the egg yolks with the sugar, ¼ cup port, and vanilla extract until hot, frothy, and thick, about 6 to 7 minutes. Allow to cool.

In a medium bowl, whip the heavy cream to a soft peak. Fold in the mascarpone and egg-yolk mixture.

Combine the espresso and remaining port in a small bowl. Soak the challah fingers in the espresso-port dip.

Place alternating layers of the soaked challah and the mascarpone mixture in a large loaf pan or trifle dish, dusting each layer well with cocoa powder. Shave chocolate over the top layer and chill at least 3 hours before serving.

Chocolate Panini

The amount of chocolate varies, depending upon which type of bread you use. The idea is to cover one piece of bread with about ⅜ inch chocolate.

SERVES 1

1   ounce premium-quality bittersweet chocolate, chopped
2   slices ciabatta bread or French bread, sliced ½ inch thick

PLACE chocolate on a slice of bread, arranging evenly and up to ½ inch from all edges to allow space for chocolate to melt. Cover with the other slice of bread.

Grill in a press until golden brown and the chocolate has melted, about 1 to 2 minutes per side. Cool briefly before serving.

ACKNOWLEDGMENTS

Panera Bread thanks the following people for their hard work and commitment in the creation of this cookbook. Without their devotion and love of this project, it would not have been possible. Gordon Albright, Scott Davis, Cheryl Hanson, Michele Kloeppel, Lisa Lorenz, Mike Marino, Teresa Muehlenkamp, Nicole Reynolds, Julie Somers, John Taylor, the staff at Teaspace, Arlene Ligori, Pascha Scott, Kevin Ament, Patrick Davis, Kristin Dormeyer, and Michael Sebastian. And of course we are ever grateful for the wisdom and direction of Pam Krauss, Jennifer DeFilippi, and the entire team at Clarkson Potter.

Thank you to our team of associates, who bring Panera warmth to all of our guests.

And finally, thank you to our team of artisan bakers for sharing their passion, craft, and art every day.

INDEX

CONVERSION CHART

equivalent imperial and metric measurements

American cooks use standard containers, the 8-ounce cup and a tablespoon that takes exactly 16 level fillings to fill that cup level. Measuring by cup makes it very difficult to give weight equivalents, as a cup of densely packed butter will weigh considerably more than a cup of flour. The easiest way therefore to deal with cup measurements in recipes is to take the amount by volume rather than by weight. Thus the equation reads:

1 cup = 240 ml = 8 fl. oz.   ½ cup = 120 ml = 4 fl. oz.

In the States, butter is often measured in sticks. One stick is the equivalent of 8 tablespoons. One tablespoon of butter is therefore the equivalent to ½ ounce/15 grams.

SOLID MEASURES

| U.S. and Imperial Measures | | Metric Measures | |
Ounces	Pounds	Grams	Kilos
1		28	
2		56	
3½		100	
4	¼	112	
5		140	
6		168	
8	½	225	
9		250	¼
12	¾	340	
16	1	450	
18		500	½

LIQUID MEASURES

Fluid Ounces	U.S.	Imperial	Milliliters
	1 teaspoon	1 teaspoon	5
¼	2 teaspoons	1 dessertspoon	10
½	1 tablespoon	1 tablespoon	14
1	2 tablespoons	2 tablespoons	28
2	¼ cup	4 tablespoons	56
4	½ cup		120
5		¼ pint or 1 gill	140
6	¾ cup		170
8	1 cup		240
9			250, ¼ liter
10	1¼ cups	½ pint	280
12	1½ cups		340
15		¾ pint	420
16	2 cups		450

OVEN TEMPERATURE EQUIVALENTS

Fahrenheit	Celsius	Gas Mark	Description
225	110	¼	Cool
250	130	½	
275	140	1	Very Slow
300	150	2	
325	170	3	Slow
350	180	4	Moderate
375	190	5	
400	200	6	Moderately Hot
425	220	7	Fairly Hot
450	230	8	Hot
475	240	9	Very Hot
500	250	10	Extremely Hot

Any broiling recipes can be used with the grill of the oven, but beware of high-temperature grills.

EQUIVALENTS FOR INGREDIENTS AND TOOLS

all-purpose flour—plain flour
baking sheet—oven tray
buttermilk—ordinary milk
cheesecloth—muslin
coarse salt—kitchen salt
cornstarch—cornflour
eggplant—aubergine

granulated sugar—caster sugar
half and half—12% fat milk
heavy cream—double cream
light cream—single cream
lima beans—broad beans
parchment paper—greaseproof paper
plastic wrap—cling film

scallion—spring onion
shortening—white fat
unbleached flour—strong, white flour
vanilla bean—vanilla pod
zest—rind
zucchini—courgettes or marrow